59
MORE
STUDIO SECRETS
FOR THE
GRAPHIC ARTIST

SUSAN E. DAVIS

NORTH
LIGHT
BOOKS

CINCINNATI
OHIO

Dedication / Acknowledgments

To Alice Foster Davis and Tom Loftin Davis
Thanks for your trust, generosity, and love

Many people helped make this book possible. Special thanks are due to:

David Lewis, Editorial Director of North Light Books, for proposing this book. It was an extremely exciting and rewarding experience, and I shall always be grateful.

Diana Martin, Acquisitions Editor, for supervising the photography and for valuable advice. Her expertise made this a better book.

William Bevington, New York City graphic designer, for reviewing the manuscript and making many helpful suggestions.

Joel Kovitz, photographer, for taking my picture.

Each of the contributors, for their willingness to give of their time and share their work to help others in the profession. I couldn't have done it without them. May abundant success be their reward for making this book a reality.

93 92 91 90 89   5 4 3 2 1

Library of Congress Cataloging in Publication Data

Davis, Susan E. (Susan Elizabeth)
   59 more studio secrets for the graphic artist / Susan E. Davis.
     p.   cm.
   Includes index.
   ISBN 0-89134-316-4
   1. Graphic arts—Technique. 2. Communication in design.
I. Title. II. Title: Fifty-nine more studio secrets for the graphic artist.
NC1000.D38   1987
741.6—dc20   89-8628
                                         CIP

Editorial development by Diana Martin.
Designed by Catt Lyon Design.
The following page constitutes an extension of this copyright page.

Permissions

The following artists have graciously granted permission to reproduce their work for use in this book.

MARK ALLISON
p 107 © 1989

JOHN ANGELINI
p 21 © 1989

PETER BAGNOLO
pp 115, 116, 117, 118 © 1989

GLENN BOOKMAN
pp 4, 5, 6, 42 © 1989

LISA BOURKE
pp 86, 87, 88, 89 © 1989

HOWARD F. BRADYBAUGH
pp 90, 91 © 1989

DEBORAH BRUMFIELD
pp 12, 13 © 1989

STEVEN CARROLL
pp 28, 29 © 1989

GISELE C. CONN
pp 10, 11 © 1989

JIM CONNELLY
pp 62, 64, 65 © 1989

SCOTT CONRAD
p 106 © 1989

BECKY L. CRAIG
p 44 © 1989

TONY DILAURENZIO
pp 18, 19, 20 © 1989

PETE DREGER
pp 16, 17 © 1989

JAMES M. EFFLER
pp 58, 60, 61 © 1989

DONALD FEIGHT
p 119 © 1989

ISABEL C. GUERRA
pp 7, 8 © 1989

W. J. HILDEBRANDT
pp 36, 37, 38 © 1989

ROBERT HUDNALL
pp 59, 102, 103 © 1989

KERRY S. JENKINS
pp 22, 23 © 1989

PETER KUPER
pp 82, 83, 84, 85 © 1989

NITA LELAND
pp 100, 101 © 1989

JOSEPH LERTOLA
pp 120, 121, 122, 123, 124 © 1989

DAVID LEWIS
pp 32, 33 © 1989

LACHLAN MCINTOSH
pp 2, 3, © 1989

RICHARD E. MCVICKER
p 109 © 1989

ANNI MATSICK
pp 112, 113, 114 © 1989

BARBARA MATUNAS
pp 14, 15 © 1989

ROSE MAYER
pp 16, 17 © 1989

MARK MEALY
pp 66, 67, 68 © 1989

DAVID MILLER
pp 58, 60, 61 © 1989

MARY ANN NICHOLS
pp 34, 35 © 1989

SHARON L. NOEL
pp 30, 31 © 1989

TOM O'LEARY
p 108 © 1989

PAUL PULLARA
p 39 © 1989

RANDALL RAYON
pp 92, 93 © 1989

MARK RIEDY
pp 72, 73, 74, 75, 76, 77, 78, 79 © 1989

LESLEY SCHIFF
pp 80, 81 © 1989

CARLA SCORNAVACCO
pp 104, 105 © 1989

LENORE SIMON
pp 96, 97, 98, 99 © 1989

WELMOED B. SISSON
p 43 © 1989

JOHN S. SLORP
p 45 © 1989

EUGENE M. SMITH, JR.
p 9 © 1989

CHRIS SPOLLEN
pp 50, 51, 52 © 1989

REED SPRUNGER
pp 24, 25 © 1989

JOHN E. THIES
pp 69, 70, 71 © 1989

CHARLES E. VADUN
pp 26, 27 © 1989

SHARON WATTS
pp 94, 95 © 1989

MARIA CARMER WEBB
pp 110, 111 © 1989

LEE WOOLERY
pp 53, 54, 55, 56 © 1989

ANGELA WOOLLEY
p 57 © 1989

DAVID PHILLIPS YOUNG
pp 40, 41 © 1989

Contents

Secret Topic Index

Introduction

What this book offers you

Working alone or in a small design studio may offer you different advantages than those you'd find in a busy ad agency or a corporate design department. Yet, no matter where you work—whether in Coos Bay, Oregon, or Lubbock, Texas, or Stone Mountain, Georgia, or Walpole, New Hampshire, or Wyoming, Michigan—you need new ideas to stimulate and energize your work. You need to recharge your creative batteries and learn new working techniques so you can stay abreast of the industry and continue producing consistent, high-quality designs.

Every graphic artist must continually improve methods of:
- Finding more innovative ways to express concepts, ideas, or visions
- Solving problems and troubleshooting
- Saving time, money, and energy

Luckily, there are lots of ways you can get help. Fresh images always trigger the creative process, so you can soak up fine art in museums or art galleries. But that takes you away from the studio, and besides, you may not have a constant flow of high-caliber shows and exhibits in your hometown.

Another way is to study other designers' work in magazines, ads, design annuals, books, and on calendars and posters. While often rewarding, that approach has built-in frustrations. How many times have you thought, But how did he or she *do* that? And other times, when you're tired, overworked, and feeling frustrated, you know there *should* be an easier, faster, less-expensive way to do the job that would let you be as efficient and productive as the artist at the next board, behind the next door, or in the next city.

How this book can help you . . .

This book was written to solve just such problems. Graphic artists should have easy access to new design and illustration ideas. You shouldn't have to search or scrounge. You should have readily available resource materials that offer creative ideas and practical, tested processes that you can easily adopt or adapt in your work.

In fact, sharing tested and useful techniques is a traditional way of encouraging high professional standards. Doctors are expected to write up research results or describe their latest surgical procedure; the practice of law is based on the study and citation of related cases. Graphic artists are still in the process of establishing credentials and criteria, so a book like this helps promote the profession's overall aims of quality and excellence—and provides a practical, valuable service as well.

The book *Studio Secrets for the Graphic Artist*, published by North Light Books in 1986, paved the way for this book. Its success showed that designers not only wanted but were eager for new ideas and techniques. While that book included basic concepts and working procedures, in addition to 12 projects, this book presents 59 design and illustration secrets contributed by 52 graphic artists. It presumes a basic knowledge of graphic design techniques and working methods.

This book features 59 ideas . . .

How this book came about—and how these particular graphic artists came to be included in it—is based on the following premise: Working designers are always experimenting in search of new techniques. Editors at North Light Books believed they could find enough good ideas from designers to produce a sequel to *Studio Secrets for the Graphic Artist*. So graphic designers were invited to "share your secrets" in a call initiated by North Light Books in the spring of 1988.

. . . contributed by 52 graphic artists

Selected from dozens of submissions, the 59 innovative concepts came from 52 graphic artists. Their techniques showed originality and had a broad enough application to be of use and interest to a wide audience. Many take advantage of technology—such as photocopiers—while others show new ways of airbrushing, using photography, or preparing a comp quickly. All the contributors are working professionals, and there are as many newcomers to the trade as there are old hands. They come from every area of the country—including all the towns mentioned above. While there are a few graphic artists and illustrators of national reputation among the contributors, most are the kind of unsung but skilled practitioners who are the bedrock of the profession.

The work is presented in two categories:
• *Design:* Section One contains those working techniques that save artists time, money, and energy, such as a variety of ways to prepare and present comps.
• *Illustration:* Section Two provides an impressive range of illustration techniques, from innovative ways to work with markers, airbrush, and technical pens to the latest technology in photography and computer graphics.

The process of creating this book reflects what's best in the profession. Fifty-two graphic artists were willing to take the time and make the effort to share their methods to help other artists. Everyone gains from the exchange. But, above all, you're the real winner.

D E S I G N

S E C R E T S

You know the old saying: "Necessity is the mother of invention." The twenty-four graphic artists in this section can testify to that. They weren't overwhelmed by a flash of genius one day. All of them discovered their secrets while trying to solve a design or production problem. Invariably, they were motivated by the need to produce work faster, easier, more technically perfect, more economically, and on time.

The twenty-six techniques in this part of the book answer a wide variety of practical needs. The section begins with nine ways to comp layouts—from a quick way to make a full-color comp to blind embossing. Eight secrets involve using a photocopier. That seems to be every designer's newest high-tech tool—and as necessary today as a drawing board or a technical pen. Several general working methods and a cache of useful mini-secrets complete the section.

1 "Instant" Full-Color Comps

Lachlan McIntosh

Graphic Designer and Writer
The Write Design
Akron, Ohio

"Clients who ordinarily have a hard time trying to visualize comps will have no trouble with this technique because it approximates finished color printing," says Lachlan McIntosh, who combines the skills of graphic designer and writer in his work on direct mail packages and other design work. "Photographers can also see exactly what you want, and you will save time by not having to do finished marker renderings."

Lachlan's secret involves mounting a Polaroid photograph on a gradated-tone background in a very tight, four-color comp. He finds this technique is very quick and effective for "comping hard goods with clean lines, such as telephones, video cassette recorders, televisions, major appliances, and furniture. It's a great timesaver when you need to show many color-photo comps in catalogs or brochures with lots of illustrations."

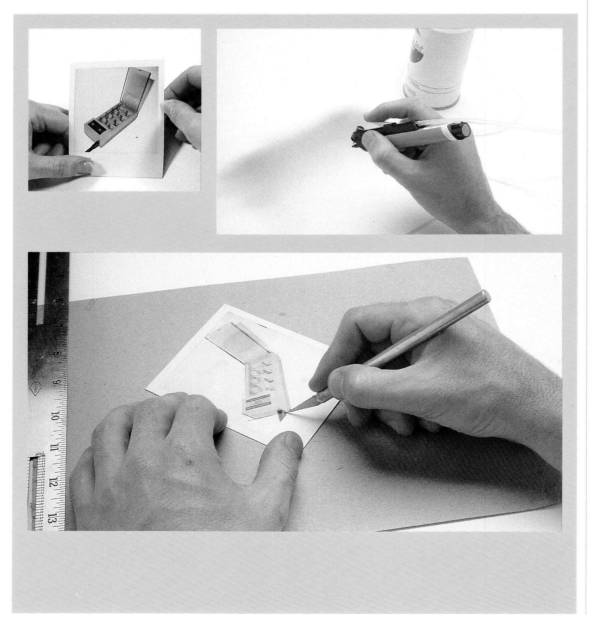

Step 1 Shoot the product with color Polaroid film and set the photo aside.

Step 2 Using a marker sprayer, create a gradated tone for a color background. Trim this background to fit your layout and attach it to your board with wax or spray adhesive. (You can also use an airbrush or the pastel technique on pages 12–13 to create the background.)

Step 3 With a sharp X-Acto knife, cut the product out of the Polaroid photo you made in Step 1. Be sure to cut deeply so that you go through all layers of the film. A metal straightedge is a helpful guide when cutting long, straight lines.

Step 4 Peel away all layers of the emulsion except the white "silvering" layer. (Without that, your photo will look flat and lifeless.) Now, spray a matte finish on the photo so that the finish will blend with the rest of the comp.

Step 5 Spray glue on the back of the photo. Wax doesn't work as well since the heat from the waxer tends to damage the white backing. Mount the photo in position on the layout.

Step 6 Your layout is now ready for client review.

A deal so good
it jumps off
the page

2 Faking a Reverse

Glenn Bookman

Graphic Designer, Illustrator, and
Product Developer
ARTWORKS Studio
Elkins Park, Pennsylvania

"Often when you're designing a layout, you want to show a client how it will look in reverse," states designer Glenn Bookman. "Instead of tediously trying to black in around intricate lettering or art, I have developed a faster, inexpensive way with cleaner-looking results." Glenn applies white china marker to areas he wants to appear white and then covers the whole design with a layer of black marker. Because the china marker repels the black, you can then wipe the black marker off the white areas. You can also use other color china markers, such as yellow or red, to achieve a similar effect.

Though this method may be more labor-intensive than some others, it may come in handy if you're working on an extremely tight budget. In fact, Glenn asserts, "This technique will help make you a more successful graphic artist because it saves time and expense (such as for reverse stats) and let's you sharpen and experiment with your concepts as you work. But most of all, it helps you present your ideas more clearly to clients. Many people have trouble trying to visualize in reverse, and a clear presentation can make the difference in whether you get a go-ahead on a project!"

(Secrets 3 and 4 show two other ways of reversing type for comps.)

Step 1 This is the art Glenn wants to show in reverse on his comp layout.

Step 2 Carefully trace an outline of the art with a pencil.

Step 3 Use a white china marker sharpened to a fine point to fill in all areas that were solid black in the original art. Press firmly on the marker to fill the paper's pores and follow the lines carefully. It helps if you keep the marker very sharp. The more thorough you are at this stage, the cleaner your final result will look.

Step 4 Go over the whole drawing lightly with a wide-nibbed black marker and let the ink penetrate. To achieve an even tone across the art, work continuously and try not to scrub the surface with the tip of the marker. The areas with the china marker will repel the black.

Step 5 There are two ways you can remove the black residue from the white borders. You can take a paper towel and rub lightly, though some areas may require firmer rubbing to remove the black. Or, if you want to make sure the white areas are very clean and sharp, take a cotton swab (as shown here), dampen it with rubber cement thinner, and gently wipe the white areas. If any spots have marker bleed or are smudged and need to be touched up, you can simply repeat the process, using white marker for white areas and black for black areas.

Step 6 Now your easy method of reversing type for a presentation comp is completed.

Isabel C. Guerra

Graphic Artist
Jersey City, New Jersey

Isabel Guerra is often called upon to do final comps in the busy New York City studio, Bevington Designs, Inc., in which she works. "Making a comp with white or colored type on a black background usually involves expensive and time-consuming transfer type, but I've found ways to do it that are simple and inexpensive." Isabel's secret ingredients in this example are transfer type and transparent tape. This method, Isabel has found, works equally well with either a solid black or a color background.

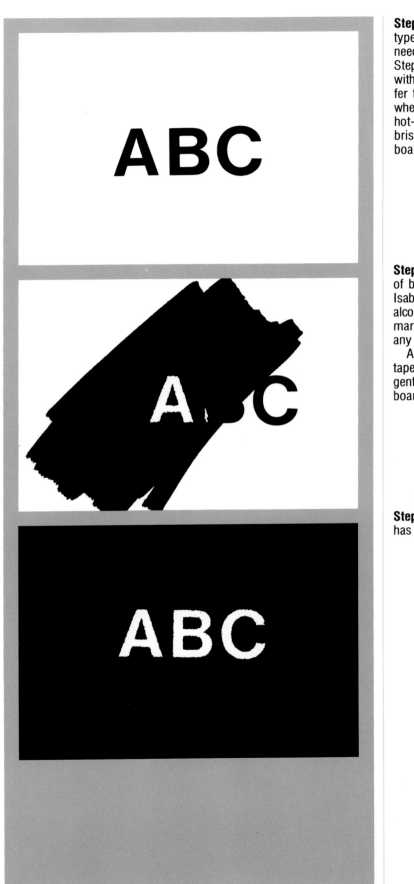

Step 1 Position black transfer type onto white paper. You'll need to pick up the letters in Step 2, so be sure to burnish with only enough force to transfer the type. This works best when the paper has a smooth hot-press finish, like that of bristol paper or illustration board.

Step 2 Apply an even layer of black marker over the type. Isabel used a waterproof, alcohol-based Faber-Castell marker here, but you could use any brand or color.
  Adhere a low-tack transparent tape to the type and begin to gently lift the letters off your board.

Step 3 Your completed comp has a finished look in minutes.

4 Reversing Colored Type

Isabel C. Guerra

Graphic Artist
Jersey City, New Jersey

Isabel must use a lot of reverse type in her designs! Here, she's come up with a simple yet very sophisticated presentation technique. "My method of shooting a film negative of a black-and-white mechanical is not only quick and inexpensive, it's also accurate," Isabel asserts. "The comp looks as good as the printed piece, allowing you to make a clean and clear presentation to the client." And if the film's glossiness doesn't suit your presentation, you can always spray the film with a matte finish.

Step 1 Lay out your comp mechanical with black type on white paper exactly as you want it to appear. Then have a film negative shot of the mechanical. Now you have clear type dropping out of a solid black field.

Step 2 If you want to show colored type in your comp, mount the film over a sheet of colored paper. If only certain areas of the type need to be colored (as shown here), you can paint those areas of the back of the film with acrylic, gouache, Plaka, or any other opaque water-based paint. (Isabel used Plaka here.) After applying a light coat of spray adhesive, you're ready to position the film in your final comp.

Step 3 If the film's glossiness isn't appropriate for your comp, spray the film evenly with a matte finish before mounting it in position.

Eugene M. Smith, Jr.

Graphic Designer
Mt. Vernon, New York

You can't use an actual transparency or 35mm slide to indicate position on a mechanical, right? All you can do is draw your holding lines, put a big *X* across the allotted space, indicate crop marks on the film sleeve, and hope the printer positions the artwork correctly. You can always correct a bad crop when checking proofs.

Here's a simpler method. Gene Smith has discovered a way to create position-only prints for transparencies or slides. Leave it to a brand-new graphic designer to devise an ingenious photocopying technique using a desk lamp with a 100-watt bulb. Instructs Gene, "Place the slide on the photocopier, but don't close the lid. Project the light from the desk lamp through the back of the slide while making a photocopy. Be careful to hold the lamp steady over the slide and keep the two a safe distance apart—anywhere from 3 to 8 inches. Using your first copy as a starting point, experiment with the light until you get the correct exposure."

Although the trial-and-error process may seem time-consuming, especially when enlarging a slide to the proper size, it can save you time at the proofing stage and money in corrections.

Step 1 Projecting a 100-watt light through the back of a slide allows the photocopier to read and record the image. You may need an assistant to help you hold the lamp steady while keeping it an appropriate and safe distance above the slide. Trial and error is essential in making this technique work.

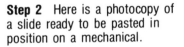

Step 2 Here is a photocopy of a slide ready to be pasted in position on a mechanical.

Gisele C. Conn

Graphic Artist
Orange County Register
Irvine, California

Whether you're selling an idea to a client or making a dummy for layout artists to follow, creating accurate and effective comprehensive layouts often requires a great deal of time and effort. Using reliable shortcuts can speed and simplify the process immeasurably. Working under tight deadlines on a major California daily newspaper, the *Orange County Register,* graphic artist Gisele Conn devised this method of flopping an image for a comp. The secret ingredient in this technique is a photocopier.

Step 1 Make a photocopy of the photo or illustration you want to flop.

Step 2 Place the photocopy right side down on the surface you want to transfer it to. Tape it in position and apply colorless blender marker over the entire surface. Be sure to cover the whole image evenly for an effective transfer.

Step 3 Burnish the copy lightly with your fingers or with a soft cloth to complete the transfer.

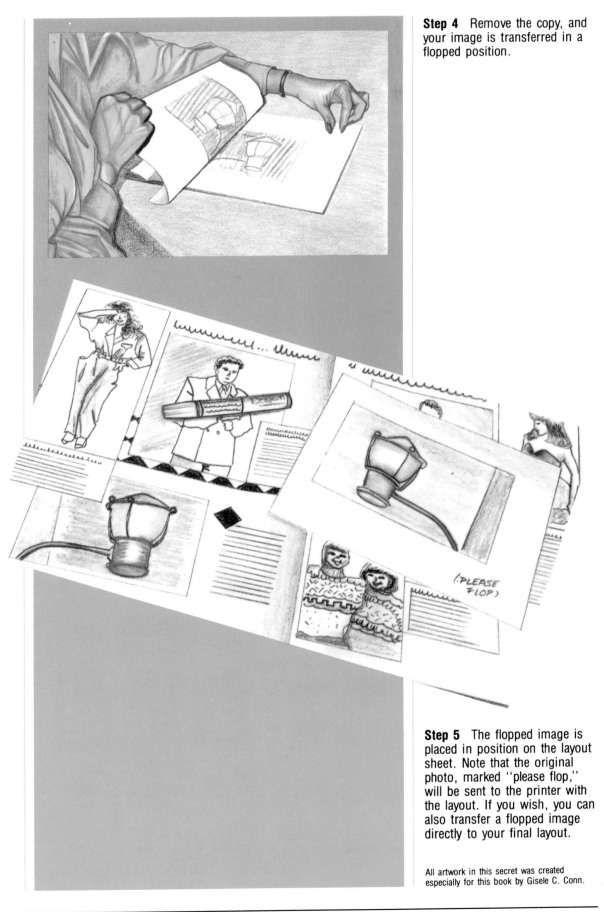

Step 4 Remove the copy, and your image is transferred in a flopped position.

Step 5 The flopped image is placed in position on the layout sheet. Note that the original photo, marked "please flop," will be sent to the printer with the layout. If you wish, you can also transfer a flopped image directly to your final layout.

All artwork in this secret was created especially for this book by Gisele C. Conn.

Deborah Brumfield

Graphic Designer
Brumfield Studios
Walpole, New Hampshire

As the owner of her own small design studio, Deborah Brumfield has learned to compensate for limited supplies and equipment by being resourceful. For one job, she needed to comp a brochure on hand-hooked rugs. She knew the background color she wanted to use—a soft peach—but she didn't have a sheet of that color paper in stock and she didn't have time to order it from the art supply store. Since she doesn't own an airbrush, she knew that she had to find another way to produce the color herself.

Deborah began experimenting with pastels and soon discovered that she could produce the effect she wanted easily, quickly, and inexpensively by rubbing shavings of pastel colors on a sheet of white paper. Whether you blend the color with your hand or a soft cloth, Deborah notes, the trick is to mix the colors in the same proportions as those listed in the PANTONE Color Formula Guide 747XR.

PANTONE®

Step 1 The color Deborah wanted to match was PANTONE 162 C, which is ½ part PANTONE Warm Red and ½ part PANTONE Yellow mixed with 15 parts PANTONE Trans. White.

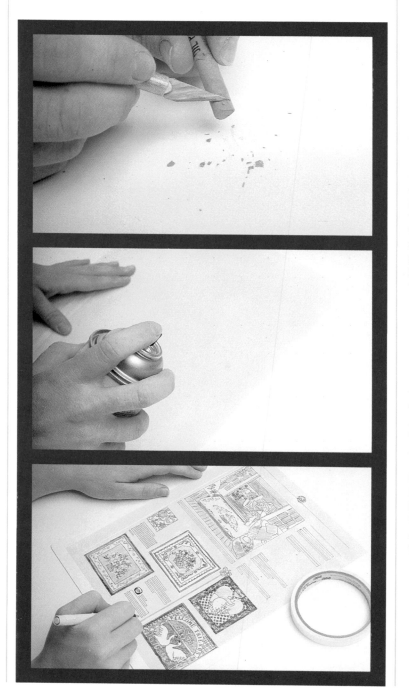

Step 2 Rather than mix the color totally from scratch, Deborah decides to save time by mixing 1 part orange pastel with 15 parts white. First she shaves a small pile of orange pastel (shown here) and then white pastel in the proper ratio onto a sheet of white paper.

Step 3 Deborah works the color into the paper using her hand until she achieves the right tone; a soft cloth works equally well. Here she sprays the entire sheet of paper with several coats of matte-finish fixative. She completed all three steps in 15 to 20 minutes.

Step 4 After mounting the colored background on a board, Deborah completes the comp. She traces the photos roughly on tracing paper, colors them with colored pencils, and sprays them with gloss varnish. Then she mounts the tissue paper on white paper, so the artwork appears opaque, and cuts and positions the art on the peach background with one-coat rubber cement. After adding greeking with her technical pen and white stripes, borders, and ornaments, the comp is ready to show the client.

NANTUCKET ISLAND • Massachusetts
Right: 47 Hulbert Avenue, Nantucket. Construction by Brant Point Corporation.

Foreground: Welcome Friends rug (described below) and Goose Runner rug (described on p. 3).

LOVE CAT
This playful friend adds a touch of happiness to your home. The wild roses of Nantucket create a striking border.
Size: 34" x 34", #CM-101.

WELCOME FRIENDS
A warm way to tell your friends they're special. Makes a great gift! Size: 33" x 43", #CM-100.

Foreground: Colonial Basket with white background (77" x 61"). Background: Spring Basket and Love Cat. (Photographed at 47 Hulbert Avenue, Nantucket. Construction by Brant Point Corporation.)

COLONIAL BASKET
Inspired by an antique colonial bed cover and charmingly adapted to brighten any room. Size: 77" x 61". #CM-107; White (above). #CM-108; Grey (on right).

SPRING BASKET
A breath of springtime surrounded by a delicate border. Delightfully versatile. Size: 48" x 60". #CM-117.

ORDER TOLL FREE
1-800-323-YARN
We accept Visa, MasterCard and American Express.

Step 5 Here is the page as it appears in the final catalog.*

*Process color reproduction may not match PANTONE®-identified solid color standards. Refer to current PANTONE Color Publications for the accurate color.

Barbara Matunas

Graphic Designer
Advertising-Marketing Resources
El Paso, Texas

Have you noticed that a limited budget often forces you to be your most creative? Graphic designer Barbara Matunas is no exception. "Since I worked for a small agency that was generally under very tight budget constraints, I had to come up with some art and design techniques for comps and presentations that used materials and equipment we had on hand. Luckily, we were able to produce quick, relatively inexpensive stats in house."

After having a stat made of her layout for a perfume package, Barbara applied Dr. Ph. Martin's Radiant Concentrated Water Colors, which she mixed to the desired color. (Luma dyes can also be used.) She added a little vinegar so the dye would adhere better to the slick repro (not fiber-based) paper. "The technique can be varied," says Barbara. "Stripes of several colors can be applied, the colors can be allowed to blend together for a rainbow effect, or you can use some tape or frisket to apply colors to selected areas."

Barbara used this technique in a number of different applications in addition to the perfume packaging shown here. For instance, she prepared a cover for a presentation booklet; she only needed a small number, but she wanted them to look custom-printed and make a strong graphic statement. She also used the technique to prepare layouts to be photographed for slide presentations. Observes Barbara, "The printed item could be an ad, flyer, brochure, book cover, package design, business card, or design for a billboard!"

Step 1 To prepare the comp of the perfume box, Barbara decides to use the following colors: lemon yellow, orange, persimmon, scarlet, and cherry red. Since she wants to control the color closely, she chooses to angle the stat so the color will run off the side. First, she applies lemon yellow dye to the lettering and the top left corner of the stat.

Step 2 Then she spreads the lemon yellow dye with a soft brush. A foam-tipped brush also works well.

Step 3 While the yellow dye is still damp, Barbara applies orange dye and then persimmon under the yellow and allows them to blend. She works quickly so a demarcation line won't form between the colors. If it does, she can add more of the lighter color and blend over the line. (If that doesn't work, she can wash the stat with clean water and begin again. If you do this, be sure not to scrub the stat too vigorously because it's easy to scratch the emulsion and ruin the stat.) Once the lettering is colored, she begins adding scarlet dye in the lower left corner.

Step 4 Working quickly, Barbara adds the deep cherry red dye to the rest of the stat. She brushes the color carefully to blend it with the other colors and even it out. If too much water is added, the color can become blotchy, but it's easy to blot puddles of color or water with a paper towel. If the color seems too light, Barbara just adds more dye until the color is the right density. After allowing the stat to dry, Barbara sprays it with a fixative. (It's best to test a fixative first on scraps of colored stat paper to make sure the color will not run.) Then she begins cutting out the outline of the box with an X-Acto knife.

Step 5 After she finishes cutting it out, the designer scores, creases, and folds the box for presentation to the client.

**Rose Mayer and
Pete Dreger**

Graphic Designers
Chicago Tribune
Chicago, Illinois

How many times have you wanted to show a client blind embossing in a presentation comp but didn't know how to do it quickly and easily? Graphic designers Rose Mayer and Pete Dreger can show you how they did it for their employer, the *Chicago Tribune*. Their technique is quite simple and straightforward. It will make your next presentation look that much more finished and professional.

Step 1   Photocopy the image to be blind embossed and tack the copy lightly with spray mount over a piece of heavy-ply cardboard. In this case the artists use a photostat of the type. (You can also use a pencil rubbing or Artograph of the image, but a photocopy or stat may be easiest or quickest.) Note that the board must be thick enough so that the embossed image can be pushed through it, but thin enough so that it can be cut with a sharp X-Acto knife.

Step 2   Carefully cut through the image and the board to create the stencil. Delicate areas may need to be simplified or thin rules exaggerated. Note that tape is used here to hold the *A* together.

Step 3   Turn the stencil over so that the image reads from right to left, instead of left to right. Place the paper you want to use over the reversed stencil, tack it in position, and mount the entire board on a light table. Using a burnisher with a fine point, push the paper through the stencil. It works best if you begin with the edges.

Step 4 Now the fake blind emboss is ready for presentation. Gold lettering and a rule have been added here to complete the comp.

Step 5 As you can see, the final printed piece looks very much like the accurate comp.

Tony DiLaurenzio

Commercial Artist
AD Art & Design
Selden, New York

Commercial artist Tony DiLaurenzio spends a lot of time preparing comps in the course of his packaging and sales promotion work. No wonder he's able to share several secrets that make the comping process go faster and more effi-ciently. "If you need cut lettering for a tight comp," Tony advises, "you don't have to transfer a tracing of the letters to colored paper before cutting. The trick is to paste the tissue of the lettering on the back of your colored paper in a *flopped* position." This secret works particularly well with larger sizes of letters.

Step 1 Apply one coat of rubber cement over the tissue and your lettering. Allow it to dry.

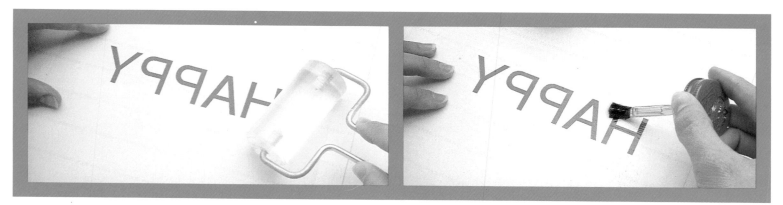

Step 2 Turn the tissue over and position it face down on the *back* of a sheet of colored paper. Burnish well.

Step 3 Apply a layer of rubber cement to the tissue. This step eliminates the need—and potential messiness—of applying rubber cement *after* the letters have been cut.

Step 4 Cut out the letters after the rubber cement dries.

Step 5 You now have self-adhesive colored letters that are ready to be laid in position on your comp layout.

Tony DiLaurenzio

Commercial Artist
AD Art & Design
Selden, New York

To center the colored-paper letters produced in Secret 10 in a layout, commercial artist Tony DiLaurenzio has devised a quick, surefire method. Centering lettering, whether for a tight comp or in a final mechanical, usually requires one part patience to two parts good planning. Yet Tony's method works every time—and eliminates the need for both guidelines and patience. The secret of Tony's success is a design tool that speeds and simplifies the process: a photocopier.

Step 1   Your original lettering can come from many sources—dry transfer, typesetting, or hand cutting, as shown here. For a clean and efficient technique, see Secret 10, Quick Cut Lettering.

Step 2   Position your lettering accurately on a sheet of paper and photocopy it. Cut the copy horizontally through the center of the letters. Place the top half of the copy in position on your layout, securing it from the top with at least two pieces of masking tape.

Step 3   Line up your cut letters, which have already been cemented (see Step 3 in Secret 10), in position over the copy.

Step 4 Burnish only the bottom half of the letters, taking care not to burnish the top half to the photocopy.

Step 5 Untape and slide out the photocopy. Now you're ready to burnish the top half of the letters.

Step 6 Your layout is finished in no time.

John M. Angelini

Artist
Hudson, Florida

A photocopier is "an experimental creative tool that is fun to work with in both fine and commercial art," says John Angelini, who has years of experience in both fields. John notes that a photocopier also saves valuable time when you have to reduce or increase the size of an image or typography. Rather than having to tediously copy a compositional element using a transfer grid, you can use the photocopier to produce the artwork needed for a comp in a matter of seconds at minimal cost. Sometimes the process may require a series of simple intermediate steps, but as John recommends, you may want to save these photocopies for other uses that may arise in the future.

A photocopier is an especially useful design tool when you need to repeat a detailed design element in a comp. John wanted six identical panels for a board game that he was creating on speculation. By using a photocopier, he was able to eliminate hours of repetitive time and effort at the drawing board.

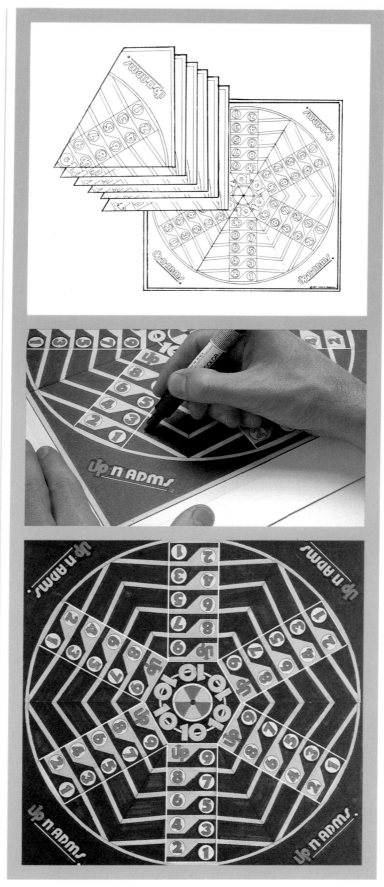

Step 1 John begins by drawing a rough sketch of one panel in pencil on tracing paper. Then he photocopies it six times at the same size.

Step 2 The artist tapes the sections together with transparent tape to make sure they fit and to check the design. It is at this stage that he makes adjustments and refinements in the design and experiments with various enlargements and reductions. He repeats Step 1 a number of times until he's satisfied. Then he makes the final comp by taping the sections together with transparent tape and rubber cementing them to a stiff board.

Step 3 John roughs out several color schemes in marker on semitransparent layout paper superimposed over one section of the layout. After choosing one color combination, the artist colors the comp with yellow and red watercolor and light blue and black marker. White lines are added with a ruling pen.

Step 4 In short order John has a finished comp.

Kerry S. Jenkins

Graphic Designer
Arthur Andersen & Co.
Charlotte, North Carolina

Under deadline pressures at Arthur Andersen & Co., an audit and accounting, tax, and information consulting firm, graphic designer Kerry Jenkins devised a quick, easy way to make tints or screens for comps or roughs using a photocopier. The process, he notes, may also be used for final art in an in-house publication.

Kerry begins with a sheet of Letratone*—in this case, he chose LT 28, which has 42.5 dots per inch and is a 70% black tint. His secret involves transforming it to a white positive. (Though the transfer process from black to white is somewhat expensive, Kerry only needs to do it once. He can keep the white sheet on file and reuse it as needed.)

Then Kerry places the white screen face down on a photocopier and positions his original black art or type face down on top of it. That produces a 30% screened image. "For best results, I usually lighten the photocopies as well. I also put several sheets of white paper on top of the original art to make sure there is tight contact between the white screen and the original art when I close the photocopier cover."

*The words Letraset®, Spacematic, Instant Lettering, and other words starting with Letra are trademarks of Letraset USA and are widely protected by legislation.

"Well done is better than well said."

B Franklin

Step 1 Here are the original artwork and type. In his final illustration, Kerry wants to show the artwork screened to a 30% black and the type 100% black.

Step 2 He has a white dry transfer made of the sheet of Letratone LT 28, which is a 70% black. This gives him a white positive version of the screen.

Step 3 Placing the white screen face down on the photocopier machine, he carefully positions the original image of Ben Franklin on top of it and sets the machine for a light copy. This 30% screened image is the result.

"Well done is better than well said."

B. Franklin

Step 4 Kerry copies the screened artwork with the black type onto three kinds of paper for different effects.

Reed Sprunger

Illustrator and Designer
Fort Wayne, Indiana

"My technique uses xerography and airbrush to produce reversed images of any graphic linework, however complex, whether it is type, logo, or illustration," says freelance illustrator Reed Sprunger. "It can be used not only for producing comps but, with a little imagination, for final illustrations as well."

Reed's secret takes advantage of the photocopier's technology, but it also requires precision and caution—so proceed at your own risk. Usually the machine lays down a powdered toner image, which is then fixed or fused with heat to the surface of the paper. "The key is to stop the photocopying process *after* the image is laid down, but *before* it goes through the fusing section of the copier," explains Reed. "The result is a perfectly formed copy that is not bonded to the surface and can, in fact, be manipulated or completely removed, according to the artist's whim. It acts as a frisket or mask for airbrushing, since you remove the toner after spraying, leaving the surface showing through."

Reed adds this note of caution: "As with almost any medium, there are certain limitations. They depend on the way your photocopier works, its size limit, the paper you use, and the color and density of your airbrushing. Timing the cutoff in Step 2 takes practice. However, since copies usually cost only pennies each, the medium is economical enough for lots of experimenting."

A related, but more complicated tip from Reed involves this technique: "Unfused photocopies have other uses too. You can copy type or art onto acetate, flop it, photocopy again on acetate, and leave it unfused. Lay this copy carefully face down in position and burnish thoroughly with a spoon. The toner will transfer completely to the paper, giving you a readable, custom rub-down image. You can then fix the toner with spray or run it through the photocopier again with a cover sheet to fuse the image."

Step 1 After making a quick keyline or photostat, position your artwork as you wish it to appear on your final comp or mechanical. Make sure your crop marks are dark, so the photocopy machine will pick them up.

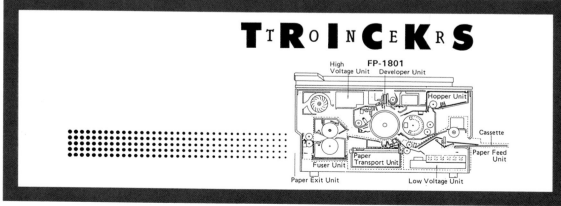

Step 2 Load the photocopier with a sheet of layout paper (Reed recommends Howard bond) and set the color contrast to dark. After positioning your artwork on the photocopier, press the button and wait as the paper is drawn through the machine. When you think it is about halfway through the process, open the photocopier door. This triggers a safety device that shuts the machine down. Flip the lever that opens the drum area and look for the copy, which should be in the section preceding the fuser. If it isn't, you'll have to start over.

Take out the photocopy very carefully; the image is very delicate at this point and most toners are highly toxic. *Be sure not to touch the drum.* Not only could you be badly burned but the machine could be damaged, requiring hundreds of dollars worth of repairs. Closing the photocopier door should reset the machine. (If you have any questions about the inside workings of your photocopier, consult your operator's manual.)

Step 3 Airbrush carefully over the image with full-strength paint and low pressure (about 15 pounds per square inch) to avoid blowing away the toner. Because the toner is not very stable, you will not be able to lay down a totally opaque layer of color. Tints work best, and any color except opaque white is recommended. Put down enough color to avoid show-through of white paper.

Step 4 Now it's time to remove the toner. Reed recommends Plasti-Tak, which is ordinarily used to stick pictures to the wall, because it picks up the toner quickly and makes a great kneaded eraser since it never hardens. You can also use a gum eraser (shown here) or masking tape, though neither is as efficient. Remove the toner with a daubing motion, and don't worry if it smears a little at this stage. It is still loose and will come up eventually.

Step 5 When you have removed enough toner for the reverse effect you wish to create, trim the artwork and spray with fixative. If you wish, you can color the reversed artwork with markers, but remember that alcohol and benzene markers smear acrylic paints. While the images produced with this technique are good enough for comps and some illustrations, they may not be sharp enough for final mechanical art. Here you can see the impact of the layout before and after portions of the toner were removed.

15 Line Art with a Halftone Effect

Charles E. Vadun

Cartoonist
San Diego, California

"I like to draw my cartoons in black ink and then shade them with gray markers," says syndicated cartoonist Chuck Vadun. "Unfortunately, this results in production problems. When the art is transferred to halftones, the crisp black lines are broken into dots. The coarser the screen, the more gray they appear in the finished work. Newspapers are the worst."

To remedy the problem, Chuck tried other techniques. He applied rub-on screens and cross-hatching to create grays, but he didn't like either effect. That's when he figured out that the secret was to preserve the best characteristics of both media: the subtle, fluid look of the marker and the density of the black ink.

"After some experimentation," Chuck relates, "I hit on the idea of putting all blacks on a sheet of clear acetate. Using the acetate drawing as an underlay, I apply the grays to a sheet of 2-ply bristol board. Then I place the acetate on top of the bristol and register the line and shade work together. That way the art can be shot separately—the blacks as line work, the grays as halftone. When composited, the finished product is identical to the original, and the client gets crisp, black outlines with a halftone effect."

Step 1 Draw your linework as usual but on a piece of clear acetate.

Step 2 Position your drawing on a light table and cover it with a piece of 2-ply bristol board.

Step 3 Guided by the linework underneath, add tone to the drawing with gray markers.

Step 4 When you are finished, place the acetate on top of the bristol board, register the two sheets, and instruct the printer to print the blacks as linework and the grays as halftone.

16 Quick, Easy Silhouettes

Steven Carroll

Senior Art Director
Decker, Kelley & Brown
Atlanta, Georgia

You know how rush-rush ad agencies are. Art director Steven Carroll came up with this technique to get himself out of a jam. He wanted to silhouette a person against a white background and vignette the bottom of the art, but his color separator didn't dot etch, there wasn't time to have the artwork retouched, and the budget was too low to allow him to use a more expensive process.

He solved the problem by having his color separator make chromalins the size of the art as it was to appear in the ad. Then he covered the art with a piece of frosted acetate and outlined individual strands of hair and ferns with a technical fountain pen. After filling in the central area of the art with a black marker, he stippled in the lower portion of the photo to create a vignetted effect. The separator then used the acetate as a window to knock out unwanted portions of the background. "It's a quick, easy method, and the results are very effective," reports Steven.

Step 1 Here is the original art that Steven wants to silhouette on the top and vignette on the bottom.

Step 2 After positioning a sheet of frosted acetate over the artwork, he outlines strands of hair with a technical fountain pen.

Step 3 After tracing the hair and all the ferns around the figure, Steven fills in the central portion of the artwork with a black ink marker. Ink or masking film could also be used.

Step 4 Then he stipples in the bottom to give the area a vignetted appearance.

Step 5 Once register marks are added, the overlay is complete.

Step 6 Here Steven silhouetted three illustrations for the final advertisement.

The designer used a variation of this technique to distinguish the spokes and details on the motorcycle's wheels. After taping a piece of rubylith over the artwork, Steven drew the spokes and outlined the wheels on the acetate with a technical pen.

Now you can love 'em and leave 'em.

The fact is, WATER GRABBER™ granules act as tiny reservoirs. They hold up to 500 times their weight in water. Just add these safe, non-toxic granules to the soil of ANY indoor or outdoor plant. Then you can water, (even fertilize), go away for several weeks and let WATER GRABBER™ care for your plants!

WATER GRABBER™ granules swell when you water, which "shakes" or aerates the soil, encouraging root growth. Then

"WATER GRABBER™ babies my beautiful begonias. They have healthy roots and bouncy blossoms."

they slowly release 95% of the water. It's water on demand for your plants. And those who enjoy watering frequently don't have to worry. With proper drainage, WATER GRABBER™ prevents waterlogging of the roots.

Thanks to WATER GRABBER™ I can water my temperamental ferns and go on a cruise with a clear conscience."

WATER GRABBER™ is just as effective for outside flower beds and vegetable gardens. The granules can even be pre-mixed with water-soluble fertilizer. WATER GRABBER™ gradually releases both water and nutrients in the soil more readily. available to roots.)

It also makes other water soluble nutrients in the soil more readily available to ...a longstanding commercial trade ...d proven by major U.S. and ...w it's finally available to ...ur plants–get WATER ...safely love 'em and leave 'em

...ram packet can absorb up to a quart of water! ...ram packets for only $2.99 let you care for ten pot plants. Or try the 69¢ introductory packet. Available at major supermarkets, plant and garden centers, and other retail outlets.

"WATER GRABBER™ takes the mystery out of watering my exotic plants and vegetables. It leaves me time for more exciting pursuits."

WATER GRABBER™

Sharon L. Noel

Graphic Designer and Artist
Shenandoah Valley Press
Strasburg, Virginia

Graphic designer Sharon Noel enjoys a challenge. Each year when the annual awards banquet of the Master Printers of America (a division of the Printing Industries of America) rolls around she gives herself another one. She tries to find another way to do an outstanding design for the banquet's program.

"In 1983 the company I work for—Shenandoah Valley Press—was awarded the printer-of-the-year award by *Newsweek*," relates Sharon. "The actual award was a fascinating sterling silver sculpture of a horse. I wanted to tie the award in with our program, but I didn't have a budget for foil stamping and I also wanted a less shiny effect. So I used thermography in conjunction with embossing. The thermography enhanced the sculptured effect and textured-silver look I wanted at the same time." Sharon notes that thermography—a process by which special powder is applied to wet ink and then heated to raise the image or type—is commonly used as an inexpensive alternative to engraving for letterheads and business cards.

All the steps leading up to the final printed piece require a 4"×5" format camera.

Step 1 Take a high-contrast photograph (shown left) of the sculpture in low light to exaggerate the contrasts in the print. (Sharon used Kodak's Tri-X Pan black-and-white 35mm film in a Canon AE-1, with a single pen flashlight as the only light source.) Have a halftone made and then use it to make an inexpensive, single-level, photo-process embossing die.

Step 2 Have a line shot made from the original photograph taken in Step 1. The line shot loses detail and holds only the areas of greatest contrast.

Step 3 Take your line shot to a print shop and ask them to "undercut" or "choke" it. In this process, used in plate-making photography, the negative of your line shot will be laid on top of unexposed film with one or more sheets of Mylar sandwiched in between. The Mylar causes the resulting image to be slightly smaller than your line shot—the more Mylar, the more light undercuts the image.

This shrinkage is intentional. Sharon explains,"I wanted to ensure that the ink didn't cover all the area to be embossed, so as to enhance the effect of a multilevel, sculpted surface."

Shenandoah's
"Lasting Impression"

Shenandoah's
"Lasting Impression"

Step 4 Using this undercut line shot, print the image. Sharon used white ink on a thick grade of gray linen cover stock.

Step 5 As quickly as the sheets come off the press, emboss them using the die made in Step 1, and sprinkle the image with silver thermography powder, which adheres only to the printed area. "This step is crucial because thermography must be done before the ink dries completely," Sharon observes. The sheets are then conveyed through a heating element. "When the covers emerge from the heating element, all the areas where the powder was applied are raised above the surface and a glossier silver is achieved than offset inks can provide. Foil stamping would have been an alternative, but that gives a shiny chrome look rather than the grainy, weathered silver I wanted here."

Sharon designed the 1984 program also using thermography. This time, unpigmented thermography powder was sprinkled lightly on brightly printed cover stock to create this grainy, airbrushed effect.

David Lewis

Graphic Designer
Terrace Park, Ohio

"The big advantage of prereleasing dry transfer lettering is that it saves time," states graphic designer David Lewis. "Someone taught me this trick when I started out doing comps for presentations 20 years ago. It's the sort of timesaver you never forget." David's only proviso is that the technique works best on straightforward type styles 24 points and larger. All you need to do it are fresh lettering, a backing sheet, a stiff ruler—and a firm grip.

Here's how the prerelease method works: Lay the sheet of lettering on a flat surface over the backing sheet. Raise the lettering, holding it firmly at the top, and with the other hand, press the ruler firmly over the letters. As you slowly slide the ruler down the letters, they will be released, turning from black to gray. David suggests you practice this several times with a sheet of old lettering to be sure you get the hang of it.

Step 1 With your lettering sheet positioned over the backing sheet, slowly press the ruler down over the letters while pulling the lettering sheet up and back with your other hand. To ensure even pressure, spread your fingers out as widely as possible along the ruler. Notice that the letters will change in color from black to gray as they're released. You must make sure that the letters are completely gray. If not, go back and do the step again.

Step 2 Holding the lettering sheet on both sides, align the needed letter—in this case *T*—over your layout and lightly press it down in place. Be sure to keep the backing sheet below your lettering line to help prevent an accidental transfer of letters.

Step 3 Prereleasing dry transfer lettering helps you complete a layout in no time.

Step 1 It's essential to be even more careful when working with ornate letters. Since it's possible for them to become broken or distorted upon transfer, check to make sure all the letter's fine lines have turned gray before lowering the ruler. After aligning the letter, use a very light touch in transferring it. Be careful to maintain the integrity of the letterform during the transfer.

Step 2 The prerelease method can be used with delicate letterforms as long as they are 24 points or larger—and you are firmly in command of the process.

These two illustrations show why it's best not to use the prerelease method with type smaller than 24 points. You won't have enough control of each letter, and there is great risk of accidental transfer of adjacent letters.

Mary Ann Nichols

Graphic Designer
Nichols Design Studio
New York, New York

Drawing perfectly rounded corners for labels, borders, letterheads, logos, or other kinds of design jobs is a chore that most designers don't look forward to with eager anticipation. New York City graphic designer Mary Ann Nichols has found a quick, easy, reliable way to do it that eliminates the urge to scream when your template slips and you have to start the drawing over for the third time!

"The secret involves drawing a circle on an Avery label. I use a circle template and a technical pen to draw a perfect circle," explains Mary Ann. "Then I slice the label in equal quarters with an X-Acto knife and position each quarter on the ruled box. This technique really saves me a lot of time and always works." You may want to experiment with this technique to see the many kinds of applications you can come up with.

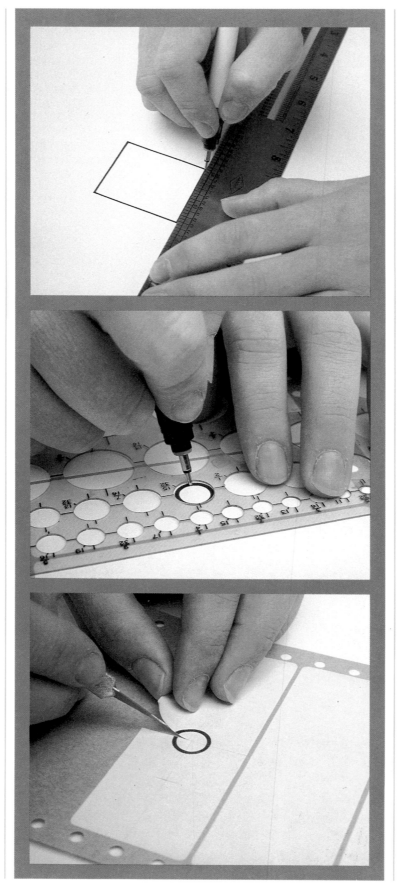

Step 1 Draw a box with a technical pen and set the box aside.

Step 2 Using the technical pen and a circle template, rule a circle on an Avery label. Make sure the size of the circle and thickness of the line fits the size and thickness of the box you drew previously.

Step 3 Using a nonreproducible blue pencil, draw perfectly perpendicular lines through the center of the circle. Cut the circle into even quarters with your X-Acto knife.

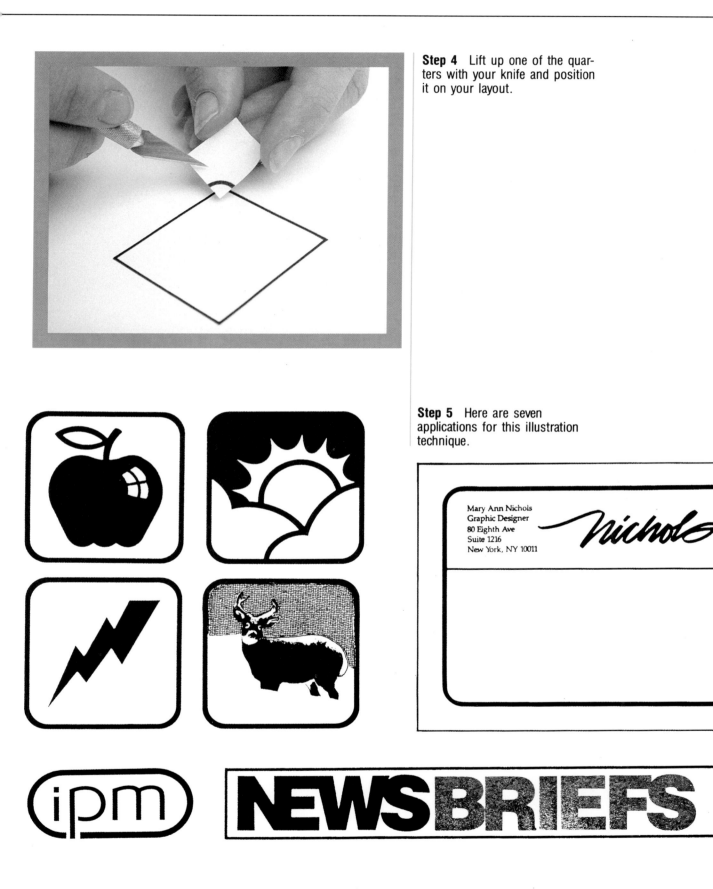

Step 4 Lift up one of the quarters with your knife and position it on your layout.

Step 5 Here are seven applications for this illustration technique.

Mary Ann Nichols
Graphic Designer
80 Eighth Ave
Suite 1216
New York, NY 10011

W. J. Hildebrandt

Calligrapher
West Simsbury, Connecticut

As a professional calligrapher, Bill Hildebrandt has to know how to position curved lines perfectly. That task often poses problems, however, for the artist or designer who is only occasionally called upon to create original lettering or position curved lines of type. Instead of bypassing an opportunity to give your work an exciting personal flourish, you can now make use of Bill's tricks of the trade. Here, he illustrates two different methods of centering curved lines: radial and parallel. You can use these same techniques equally well when centering curved lines of type.

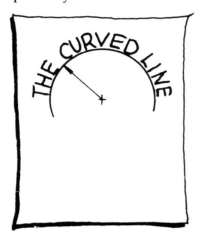

A small radius is fine for some curved lines, though it is generally hard to read. While it works for radial lines, its usefulness is limited for parallel orientation.

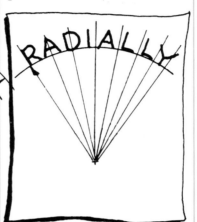

A larger radius for a curved line is easier to read. Drawing light guidelines in two concentric circles helps you maintain uniform letter height.

Curving parallel letters remain perpendicular to a common center.

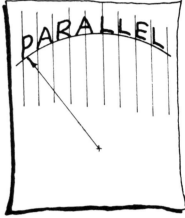

Curving radial letters are angled out from a common center.

CENTER LINE OF
LETTERING

Centering Radial Lines

Step 1 On a sheet of tracing paper, lay out two arcs as guidelines for your letters. Then write the words in the guidelines, angling them out from a common center point. Locate the center line of the lettering.

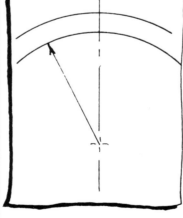

Step 2 On your final illustration board, lightly draw two guidelines for your letters and a center line.

Step 3 Place your board on a light table to do the final lettering. Cut out the lettering template and tape it in position under the board. Now you can ink over the lettering easily and quickly.

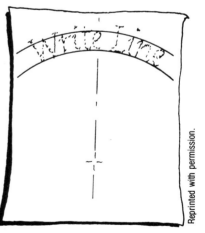

Step 4 For an alternate process, transfer the lettering to your board by using transfer paper or by rubbing a pencil over the back of your template. Burnish the letters over your board and ink.

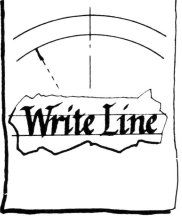

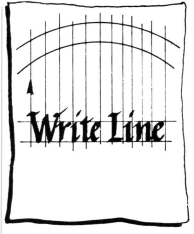

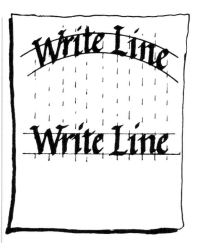

Centering Parallel Lines

Step 1 On a sheet of tracing paper, write the letters in the proper size between straight guidelines, practicing as many times as necessary until the letters are perfectly shaped and spaced.

Step 2 After drawing curved guidelines on your final illustration board and locating the center line, cut out the lettering on tracing paper, center it correctly on the board below the guidelines, and tack it lightly in position with tape.

Step 3 Project letter locations up to the curved guidelines with vertical lines.

Step 4 Ink in the final lettering, locating the correct position of each letter along the projection lines.

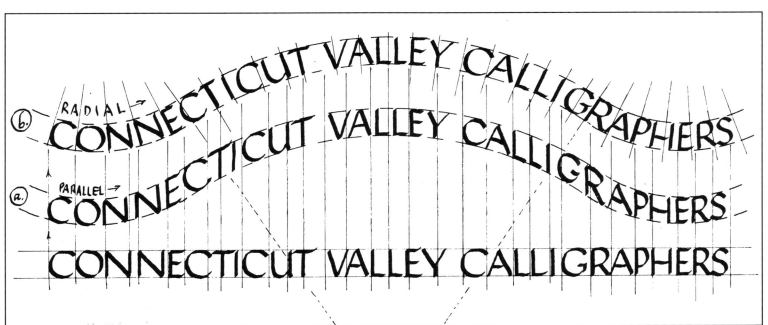

For compound curves, you must first use the parallel method to locate the letters as in *a*. But after the letters are properly located, you can write them radially as in *b* with some slight optical adjustments in spacing.

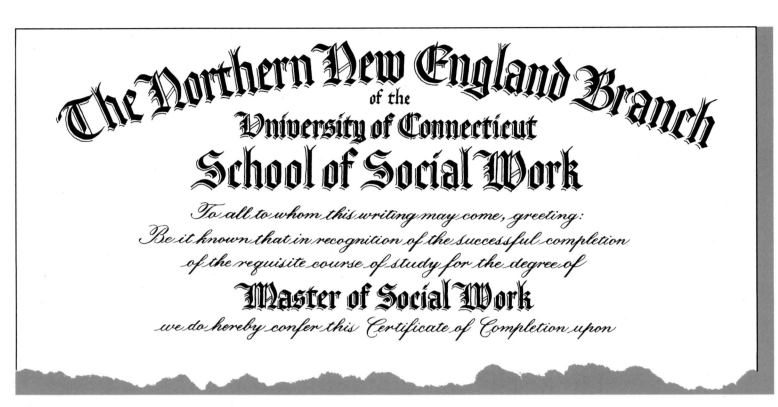

Calligraphy is often used on official documents like the degree shown here, which is an example of radially curved lettering.

Ceremonial papers are enhanced with beautiful lettering. This example shows curved letters arranged in parallel formation.

Paul Pullara

Graphic Designer
Little Falls, New Jersey

"I hate doing mechanicals, so I'll try anything that will save time and effort," admits designer Paul Pullara. "I try to keep the handling of large photostats or type repros (8"×10" and up) to a minimum, so I want to make sure that I position them right the first time."

Paul's secret is so simple you'll wonder why you didn't think of it. Before you apply rubber cement, you position the artwork and tape it along one edge, thus creating a hinge. That way you don't have to deal with art that, notes Paul, "seems to have a mind of its own, sticking where and when *it* wants."

Step 1 Before you trim your large photostat or type repro, position it on your mechanical. While holding it in position, apply a piece of tape (either masking or white artist tape) along one edge. Taping it at the top is often easiest, but that may vary depending on your mechanical.

Step 2 Flip the stat or repro over, using the taped edge as a hinge, and apply rubber cement to the back. Let it dry.

Step 3 Now carefully flip your stat or repro back to the original position, making sure not to let it buckle. It should line up exactly where you had it in Step 1. Burnish it, working down from the taped edge to release any air pockets. To protect the stat, you can lay a piece of tissue over it before burnishing.

Step 4 Remove the tape and trim the artwork to the desired size. With this method you can finish your mechanical quickly without having to contend with an unruly stat or repro.

David Phillips Young

Graphic Designer
Covington, Kentucky

With extensive experience in advertising design, graphic designer David Phillips Young has developed cost-effective techniques to meet his clients' many advertising needs. For instance, when the Waterfront Restaurant hired him to design a black-and-white newspaper ad, he knew the client might also ask him to produce other corresponding advertising materials like flyers and posters. So he created the ad with other applications in mind. He selected a format that could easily be enlarged, and he made sure that the design would work equally well reversed so he could add color later. Young's planning paid off. When the client asked him to design a small number of posters, table tents, and flyers for use at the restaurant, he was able to quickly supply very tight comps that worked well.

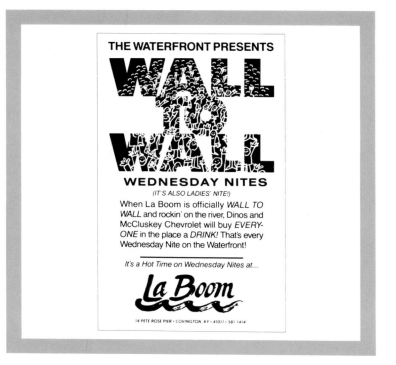

Step 1   This is the newspaper ad David has designed. He has planned it so it will be flexible enough for him to reverse it later. He has also chosen dimensions for the ad that can be enlarged to an appropriate poster size.

Step 2   This flyer has been printed in a second color for use as a small handout in the neighborhood around the restaurant. The reversed design works well with only two colors.

Step 3   To create this poster, David has enlarged and reversed the ad, mounted it on foam core, and airbrushed color over the white lettering with the aid of some frisket. Now he colors in the people with marker.

Step 4 So the poster can be mounted publicly, the designer has protected the surface with a light coat of fixative. The eye-catching poster is ready with a minimum of additional design time.

Step 5 David reduced the basic design for the table tent and added color with markers. It, too, was mounted on foam core.

Glenn Bookman

Graphic Designer, Illustrator, and Product Developer
ARTWORKS Studio
Elkins Park, Pennsylvania

As an extension of his graphic design business, Glenn Bookman has begun developing new products for the gift and novelty industry. Among his latest projects are refrigerator magnets that he models out of soft clay. "When you're working in clay, especially when you're working in miniature, there are limitations to how smooth you can get the surface and how much clean-looking detail you can work into the piece," Glenn reports. His secret is that "by applying a wash of rubber cement thinner with a cotton swab or a brush, you can get amazing results. The thinner briefly softens the surface, and with just the right touch, you can manipulate the material to produce whatever effect is needed."

Step 1 Glenn has roughed the little Santa bear out of a chunk of soft Roma Plastilina clay. Delicate finishing is needed to eliminate various tooling marks and other surface imperfections. Other versions of the bear are shown at left.

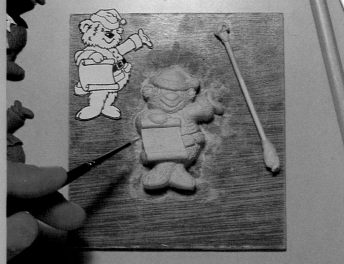

Step 2 First, the designer applies a wash of rubber cement thinner with a cotton swab and then adds more detail with a pin. Now he uses a small brush loaded with thinner to smooth out, blend, and refine various areas. By carefully manipulating the brush tip, the artist can achieve a great deal of detail and expression.

Step 3 Note the high degree of refinement Glenn was able to achieve in the finished model. This is ready to be made into a master mold from which castings will be taken. The castings are handpainted before they are put on the market as refrigerator magnets.

Welmoed B. Sisson

Graphic Artist
Flying Dutchman Design
Germantown, Maryland

Graphic artist Welmoed Sisson came up with a working technique that saves her firm both time and money. "Using dry-wipe marker boards for initial sketches for logo designs and other concepts has saved us reams of tissue paper," Welmoed explains. "Instead of sketching on a pad of vellum, we use the dry-wipe board for the first stages of design. Discarded ideas can be wiped away with a dry tissue, and the board can be reused infinitely."

"If we come up with an idea we want to develop further," Welmoed elaborates, "we can put the board in the photocopier and produce a hard copy of the image; then wipe off the board and start over. We often use these copies as 'first concept' sketches to show the client. By erasing unwanted illustrations, we're able to avoid paper clutter and having to shift through discarded sheets to find a particular sketch." Also, she notes that "each board costs us only a few dollars, and the only continuing expense is the markers, which run about a dollar apiece."

Step 1 Dry-wipe boards are excellent for playing around with ideas during the first stages of a design project. Note the light grid on the one shown here.

Step 2 Unproductive ideas can be erased with a dry tissue, and the designer avoids having to discard endless sheets of used tracing paper.

Step 3 When the designer likes a concept, it's easy to copy the sketch on a photocopier. Welmoed notes that these copies are often the first sketches shown to her firm's clients.

Step 4 Here's the final logo.

Becky L. Craig

Artist and Designer
Atlanta, Georgia

If you're frustrated because the nonreproducible blue pens you use keep smudging and smearing on your boards, Becky Craig has the perfect solution for you. Mix Dr. Ph. Martin's turquoise blue watercolor ink with water in a ratio of 10:1 and load it into a technical pen. "Now I get crisp nonphoto blue lines every time," Becky observes. "I can measure off spaces evenly too!"

Step 1 You need a new or well-cleaned technical pen and a bottle of Dr. Martin's turquoise blue watercolor. Becky mixes her ink in an old ink bottle, but you can mix it directly in the pen's reservoir or a disposable cartridge if you wish.

Step 2 Mix 1 drop of turquoise blue to 10 drops of water. When mixing a large batch, you can use 1 full dropper of Dr. Martin's to 10 full droppers of water.

Step 3 Now you're ready to fill your pen. Because the nonreproducible ink is mostly water, it won't clog the pen.

Step 4 The technical pen (below) produces a perfect, very sharp, thin line every time.

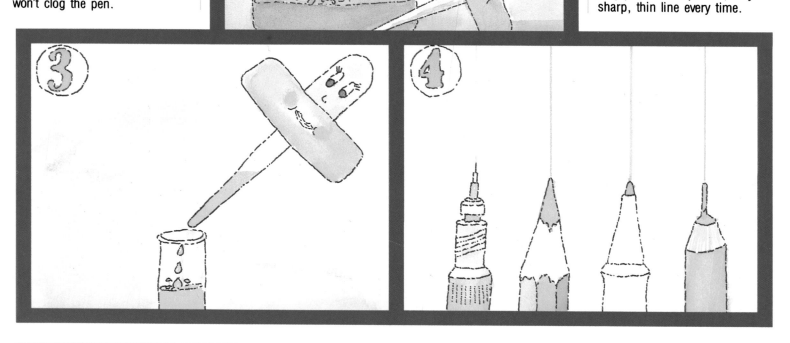

John S. Slorp

President
Memphis College of Art
Memphis, Tennessee

Do you want to add a fresh dimension to your work? How about one-of-a-kind graphic effects? With John Slorp's technique, you can make a special screen from any low-resolution halftone, pattern, or texture and apply it in a host of creative ways to letters or shapes. "Dramatic effects can be obtained from many different sources," notes Slorp, president of the Memphis College of Art, who paints and creates computer graphics in his spare time. Some of the unusual materials Slorp has used for this technique are lace, maps, and natural textures like wood grain. "You can take varied scalings of textures and pictorial matter and modify them in unique ways to enliven any project." Slorp notes that the headline type shown here was prepared on an Apple Macintosh SE and then printed with a computer-generated graphics pattern.

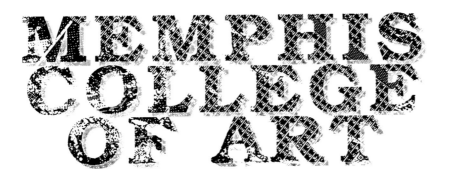

Step 1 Create a headline with rub-down letters, type, or copy composed on a computer. This technique works best with larger, bolder sizes of type. Make a film negative of the headline type. You can also make a computer reversal with a laser printer, which is printed on Mylar film.

Step 2 Select a picture, pattern, or texture. For this example, Slorp chose a graphic pattern he created on an Apple Macintosh SE computer. Have a film positive made.

Step 3 You could also reverse the artwork shown in Step 2 and use a negative of that image. Assemble the two pieces of film from Steps 1 and 2. You may vary the technique depending on which layer you put on top. Top with a rubylith mask to isolate the image area. You can send this film sandwich directly to the printer or paste a stat of the patterned lettering in your mechanical.

Step 4 This example shows the unusual effect that can be created with original artwork. Note that John has added a drop shadow to the pattern by manipulation on the computer. In addition, the overlay has been retouched (for example, the *A* and the last *E* in COLLEGE); sometimes an area may require slight retouching to maintain the integrity of the letterform.

While the twenty-six secrets featured in this section describe and illustrate innovative design ideas in several steps, some designers submitted great ideas that didn't require elaborate explanations. Here is a bonus section with twelve general working tips and techniques sure to enhance your design skills.

Checking Color at Home

Doreen Curtin
Artist, Illustrator and Designer
Clinton, New Jersey

Versatile graphic artist Doreen Curtin designs a lot of color brochures and posters, but she doesn't always have time to travel an hour or more each way to a printer to check color keys or chromalins. So she has devised a way to check them at home. "My gardener husband has Vita-Lite fluorescent bulbs in the cellar to help his seedlings grow, and he suggested I try the lights to check last-minute chromalin proofs," reports Doreen. "They work wonderfully. For the cost of a shop light and two natural-spectrum bulbs, I am now able to check work at home. Since the printers I work with provide courier service, I can complete the infamous rush job with ease. Furthermore, since I'm not always able to set aside the better part of a day to run around to a printer, this 'discovery' makes my life less frantic and therefore more productive and efficient."

Doreen notes that if you work with printers that don't provide couriers, the cost of overnight delivery service is modest enough to still allow you to work at home.

Color Coding X-Acto Knives

Carol Hettenbach
Graphic Designer/Photographer
Santee, California

"I got tired of grabbing for an X-Acto knife and picking up the wrong one," explains graphic designer Carol Hettenbach, who likes to use at least two knives, one with a standard sharp point and one with an angled edge. That's what led her to devise a simple system of color coding her knives.

First Carol tried painting different colors on the knife holders—red for the sharp no. 11 blade, blue for the angled no. 16 blade—but the paint soon chipped or rubbed off. Then she tried tape on the knife holders, but it became sticky and got in the way. Finally, she discovered some inexpensive plastic handles in the art supply store that are light and easy to use. In addition to the red and blue handles, Carol has added a third—yellow for any special blade her work might require. "You'd be surprised how this simple idea saves time and helps the work flow more smoothly," Carol admits. "As an added advantage, the handles are shaped so the knives won't roll off the drawing table."

Oil on Troubled Ink

Jack Tremblay
Graphic Artist
Rowley, Massachusetts

Graphic artist Jack Tremblay now uses disposable technical pens, but he used to get frustrated when ink would stick to the sides of the capsule in his refillable technical pen and he couldn't see how much ink he had left. If you have that problem, Jack has a solution. Put a drop of baby oil in the ink capsule before filling it. That keeps the ink off the sides, and you can easily monitor the ink level.

Controlling Glue

Kathy Dodd
Artist
Dallas, Texas

Putting thinned rubber cement in an oilcan makes gluing small pieces of type much easier, claims artist Kathy Dodd, who has used this trick for over 20 years. You can control the amount of glue—from a thin line to as broad as the end of the oilcan spout—by the amount of pressure you exert on the trigger and the speed with which you move the can.

Kathy notes three things that make this trick successful: (1) Use a new oilcan. She's found that if you don't, there's enough oil residue left in the can even after thorough washing to make the glue so gooey that it's unusable. (2) Buy an oilcan with as short a spout as possible; the longer the spout, the faster the glue dries out. The spout should not be flexible. (3) Don't set the glue can in a sunny spot or leave it on a light table. If it gets too hot, the rubber cement will expand and glue will drip from the spout.

Instant Design Tool

Steve McCue
Art Instructor
Tucson, Arizona

As an imaginative high school art instructor, Steve McCue likes to experiment with unusual ways of creating artwork. He enjoys the challenge and, at the same time, teaches his students to be inventive and adventurous. One way he found to create an instant design tool is to fashion your own brand or stamp out of 16-gauge baling wire. Just keep a small amount of wire and needle-nosed pliers handy, and you can design a stamp in minutes. (Steve chose to work with 16-gauge baling wire because it's easy to bend and retains its shape after extensive use. It helps if you leave enough wire for a handle.)

Then you're ready to print anything requiring a repeat pattern with paint or ink from a stamp pad. Varying the amount of paint and pressure on the stamp, plus changing its direction, can help you create different effects. Steve notes that the stamp is also good for making impressions in clay.

Watch Those Knives!

Stan H. Covington, Jr.
Retired Designer
Colonial Heights, Virginia

"I've seen several graphics people impale their legs or feet with a runaway X-Acto knife," states retired designer Stan H. Covington, Jr. "To safeguard against such accidents, I place a no. 2 spring clip over the blade when it's not in use and encourage my co-workers to do the same. The clip makes it roll-proof; if the knife is dropped, the clip protects both the blade and the user; and it also provides a handy hanging hole." Stan recommends the Bulldog brand of clips, which are most affordable.

Clean Edges with Removable Tape

Martha Galuszka
Art Director
Tri-Media Advertising
Newington, Connecticut

Art director Martha Galuszka has found several practical uses for clear, removable Scotch-brand transparent tape. "I have been using it instead of masking liquid or films for small areas in airbrush paintings, for making clean edges around artwork, and for keeping fingerprints off mechanical boards until the artwork is finished. And it really helps when I'm greeking justified copy. I just slide the T-square down and zip the pen back and forth really fast, and I don't have to worry about where every line ends. Also it works great to keep markers within the edges of a comp; lines are cleaner and there's no dark spot at the end of each line." Martha also notes that the tape stays in position where it's placed, is easy to cut into fine friskets, and doesn't leave a residue like other tapes.

Another Use for Removable Tape

Mark Mealy
Designer
Greenwell Goetz Architects
Washington, D.C.

If you try to pick up Zipatone that has been applied to Mylar, it leaves a sticky residue. Erasing it makes a mess, and using a solvent is overkill, as designer Mark Mealy notes from experience. To solve this problem, Mark discovered that clear, removable transparent tape works best. Just rub it thoroughly over the area, lift the tape, and the residue is gone.

Hold That Rubber Cement Jar!

Deborah Brumfield
Graphic Designer
Brumfield Studios
Walpole, New Hampshire

Graphic designer Deborah Brumfield discovered an unlikely object that keeps a rubber cement jar from sliding off an angled drafting table—a standard vacuum cleaner belt! Bought at any well-stocked hardware or department store, it fits loosely at the base of the jar so you needn't use a taboret to hold the jar. Don't ask how Deborah figured this one out—it's a long story, beginning with frustration and ending with ingenuity. In addition, she finds that small pieces of rubber cut in circles and squares also prevent knives, pens, bottles of correction fluid, and triangles from slipping off the board.

Speedy Grids

Robin Kappy
Designer and Illustrator
New York, New York

Designer and illustrator Robin Kappy has come up with a shortcut for ruling grids on layout boards. On her drawing board, she places strips of white masking tape that outline the horizontal and vertical dimensions of the layout boards. Then she marks off the grid dimensions on the tape along the two axes. In no time she has ruled neat, perfectly drawn grids and is ready to begin her layouts.

Shortcut for Flopping Line Art

Glenn Bookman
Graphic Designer, Illustrator and Product Developer
ARTWORKS Studio
Elkins Park, Pennsylvania

If you need to flop line art, Glenn Bookman's secret of photocopying art on a sheet of clear acetate simplifies the process. Then you just flip the acetate over and make a copy on white paper. Your line art is now flopped. (See Secret 50 for a description of how to photocopy on frisket.)
"Usually, to get a flopped image of line art," Glenn says, "you have to trace the original, turn over the tracing, and ink it in, which is tedious and often doesn't yield an exact duplicate. This technique ensures an exact copy in less than half the time."

Darker Copy in a Hurry

Robert Andraschko
Graphic Arts Instructor
La Crosse, Wisconsin

If you're working against a tight deadline, your photo-typeset copy is too light, and there's no time to send out for darker copy, here's an emergency solution. Go over the light copy with a yellow felt-tip marker. This will darken it enough so that it can be shot. The camera will not pick up the yellow. Robert Andraschko learned this neat trick while in the newspaper business, but he says it can be used in any situation where time and money are in short supply and reproduction quality is not critical.

N **S** E C R E S

You're always looking for fast, new, surefire ways to make your work visually expressive and appealing—not to mention finishing a particular job within budget and on time. The value of the techniques presented in this book is that you know they have been tried and tested until they work. The contributors are practicing professionals who are willing to share secrets of their success with you.

This part of the book comprises thirty-three secrets. Beginning with marker and airbrush techniques, the section also includes new ways of using a photocopier, fine art work, photography, and a variety of other techniques including computer graphics. The range of work is excitingly diverse. For example, among the illustration techniques are ways of:

• Creating art with a color laser photocopier
• Assembling a collage of images photocopied on different pieces of colored paper
• Enlarging a fine art sketch to a finished watercolor
• Using a photocopier to reproduce a sketch in blue ink, which can then be perfectly traced in black ink
• Making a highly accurate drawing from a photograph, which in the process improves drawing skills
• Creating a three-dimensional image on a computer

Some artists are highly innovative—like airbrush artist Jim Connelly, who found a way to use the household spray cleaner Fantastik to make unusual background treatments. Others are very practical—like graphic designer Carla Scornavacco, who used a photocopier to create an accurate drop-shadow effect. All are detailed here to help you be a better working professional.

Chris Spollen

Illustrator
Moonlight Press
Staten Island, New York

Award-winning illustrator Chris Spollen has developed a number of high-speed techniques over the past 15 years. "When time is tight," says Chris, "an image can be inked on vellum with technical pens and templates, giving you tight, clean edges associated with a high-contrast illustration style. To save time, rather than use a brush and ink to fill in black areas, I've found that an indelible red Pentel pen fills in and bleeds up to the inked edges, thus saving half the time it would take regular ink, applied with a brush, to dry. The red permits you to see the area you're covering better, since it contrasts with the black outline, and since it's indelible, you can work the area almost immediately."

Step 1   Chris prepares a rough pencil sketch for an oil company ad.

Step 2   This slightly modified stat is presented to the client for approval. The art director requests that the illustrator enlarge the hand holding the flag on the left.

Step 3 The illustrator lays a sheet of inking vellum over the stat and outlines the basic forms in black ink using a technical pen and drafting tools. Then he begins to fill in areas with a red Pentel pen.

Step 4 After edges are cleaned up with Letraset rub-down white lines, the vellum drawing is complete. Note that the hand has been enlarged and all areas are refined at this stage.

Step 5 After Chris makes a black-and-white stat of the vellum drawing, so he can work on a clean surface, he does more refining with red Pentel, white paint, and Letraset rub-down white lines. This process is repeated once or twice more, depending on the stage of refinement desired.

Step 6 The final artwork is ready for submission to the client. It is scheduled to appear on banners at stadiums and racetracks around the country.

Chris did this illustration of a 1930s plane, *Seaplane by Moonlight,* as a promotion for his studio. In addition to using the inking method described here, Chris applied tints of Koh-i-Noor color with a technical pen to the sky and water to create a nighttime effect.

Lee Woolery

Illustrator
Kettering, Ohio

No other drawing medium offers the impact and immediacy that can be achieved with art markers. And they speed up the creative process. You can sketch an image quickly in color without having to stop to mix paint. You can use bold strokes to capture movement or to create textures and patterns. And you can glaze colors to create subtle value changes, different moods, or even transparency. A master with art markers, illustrator Lee Woolery shows you the fundamentals—how to lay in flat color and glazing—before proceeding to a more complicated project of rendering a sleek sports car.

Laying in flat color is a marker skill you must master. You must be able to control the color, so it doesn't bleed outside your image and ruin your drawing. Staying about 1/16 inch inside your image with a broad nib marker and 1/32 inch with a fine nib will help you control excessive bleeding. It will also help

to work with a light touch.

When applying color, the objective is to keep a wet working edge to avoid creating obvious lines between strokes. That means you must work quickly, blending the strokes before they dry. Once you define an image's outline, fill in the area with overlapping diagonal strokes.

Any size area, no matter how large, can be covered with smooth, flat color if you follow the basic rule of outlining and then filling in with

overlapping strokes. The best way to learn the technique is to work freehand rather than with a straightedge guide.

Glazing makes for professional marker rendering. The technique requires that you layer color to develop your values. The more layers, the darker the value. Since the range of colored markers on the market is limited, rendering subtle value changes means that you need to know how to glaze.

Alcohol-based markers work best because you

can build up value without color pickup. This occurs whenever you stroke over a darker tone and the nib picks up the darker color. Sometimes several strokes are needed for the darker color to wear off the nib.

To practice outlining and filling in, begin by laying in an even stroke of color with the broad end of a 50% gray marker. Start at the top of a square, like the one shown here, and then do the left side, forming an inverted ''L'' shape. Fill in diagonally, making sure to overlap strokes quickly while the ink is wet. When you're nearly finished, lay a line along the bottom and one up the right side, and fill in the rest of the square.

Practice glazing by rendering a rectangle in four values of gray: 20%, 30%, 40%, and 50%. Starting on the right, lay in flat color with a 20% gray marker with a broad nib. When you are a quarter of the way across the rectangle and the 20% is still wet, switch to a 30% gray. Complete half the rectangle. Then quickly shift to the 40% gray marker while the 30% is still wet and finish that quarter. Complete the rectangle with a 50% gray marker.

Rendering a Sleek Sports Car

Rendering reflective and transparent surfaces with markers is tricky, so that makes drawing the painted car body, glass, and matte aluminum trim of a sports car a real challenge. There are plenty of elements here on which you can test or refine your marker skills. Don't worry if your first attempt doesn't come close to this expert drawing. Each time you try it, you're bound to improve.

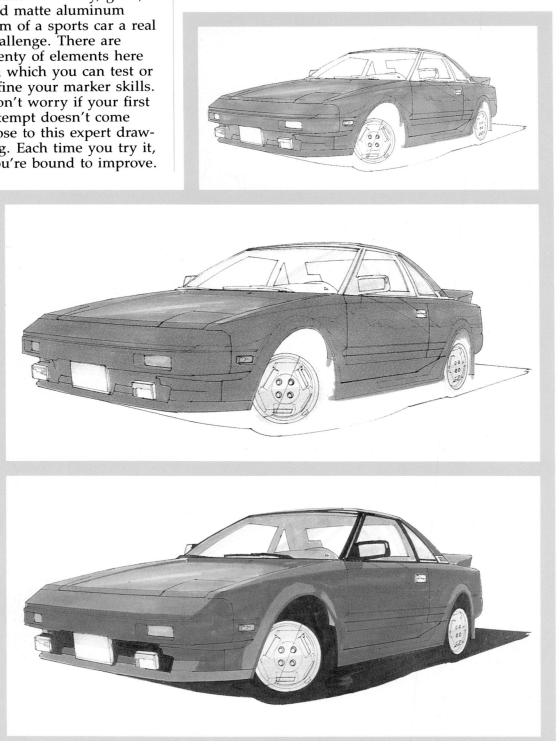

Step 1 After roughing in your sketch, begin with apple blossom on the painted surface. (The color names are those of Berol Prismacolor markers.) Use a fine point for the outline and tiny areas; fill in with a broad nib. Be sure pigment doesn't bleed into the windshield, wheels, or other areas.

Step 2 Working up from the ground, fill in the wheels with a fine-point cold 10% gray marker, switching to a cold 30% gray for the bottom half. Use an orange fine point for the parking lights and turn signal. Since all the glass areas reflect the sky, use a fine-point nonphoto blue for the fog lights, windshield, and driver's window. Also apply blue for the mirrors and window molding. To create the shadowed portion of the car body, apply a second layer of apple blossom.

Step 3 Now working from the top down, apply a cold 50% gray with a fine point to the trim and molding inside the passenger area. To add more definition to the body's shaded side, use your fine point to apply a layer of scarlet lake. Now with a black fine point, carefully fill in the area around the fog lights and license plate, the wheel wells and tires, and the shadow under the car. Then add more precise details with the black fine point—on the wipers, mirrors, window trim, and molding. Use a French curve as a guide around the molding.

Step 4 Again working from the top down, use a cold 70% gray fine-point marker to fill in the interior, window trim, door handle, mirrors (keeping the blue at the top), and the tops of the license plate and fog lights. Using the same marker, cast a shadow across the front wheel and fill in the back one, making sure to leave a light area at the rear. To define the horizontal reflection across the door, stroke a cranberry marker along the body. With the same marker, add shadows under the bumper, inside the turn signals, and shooting down from the driver's mirror. Add black areas in the wheels and in the turn signal's trim with a fine point.

Step 5 Now it's time to add all the tiny refinements that mark a professional rendering. Begin by adding grape to the deep shadows under the door and bumper and inside the turn signals. Fill in trim, mirrors, and interior seats with a cold 70% gray fine point. Switching to a cold 50% gray, create shadows in the recesses in the front wheel and turn signals, on the fog lights, and around the license plate. Add an accent on the door handle with a black fine point, and rule lines on the side molding with a straightedge. Still using the black, do the trim inside the car. With a light violet fine point, add a streak of reflected color across the windshield and driver's window.

Step 6 To create the white reflections on the windshield and door glass, you'll need to use Dr. Ph. Martin's Bleed-Proof White on a no. 0 brush. Let that dry thoroughly before carefully going over the black showing through the windshield's left side with a sharp, white Prismacolor pencil. Then trace the pencil lightly across the top of the windshield and along the areas touching the painted highlights. To finish the rendering, add white pencil lines around the doors, hood, signals, and headlight covers using a French curve.

Lee Woolery

Illustrator
Kettering, Ohio

You can render *any* textured surface with markers. It just requires careful study of a given texture's characteristics. You need to analyze the texture's components to plan the different layers of your illustration. For instance, after laying in a base tone, you need to add grain in wood and cracks and pits in concrete. Choosing the appropriate marker for each element is essential. Here, expert marker illustrator Lee Woolery provides four examples of different surfaces: wood, brick, concrete, and plaid fabric.

For wood, be sure to pick a light brown for your base tone and mix it generously with yellow. Draw the grain with a fine-point darker brown marker, making sure to add swirls and knots in the wood pattern. Add highlights with a white pencil.

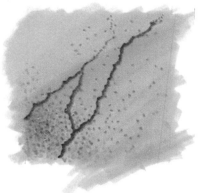

Sketch the bricks in pencil. Then overlap red dots, gradually deepening the red value along the brick's outer edges. To add mortar between the bricks, use a light gray marker and add shading along the brick's sides with darker fine-point markers.

To render concrete, lay down a base tone of warm grays and add yellow highlights. Select a darker gray to indicate the cracks and pits in the rough surface. To emphasize the sides of the cracks and create a more three-dimensional effect, apply white colored pencil to these areas.

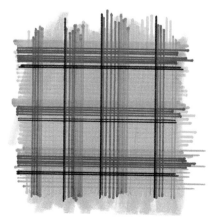

Begin this plaid fabric pattern by laying in a base tone of light blue. To add a layer of fine horizontal and vertical lines, choose several colors of fine-point markers—Lee uses orange, blue, purple, and black here—and rule them in with a T-square and triangle.

Angela Woolley

Graphic Artist
Northridge, California

Interest in photography prompted graphic artist Angela Woolley to find a way to hand-tint black-and-white photos, which she has since used in ads, comps, and storyboards. First, she tried using dyes but found them too messy and painstaking. Then she began experimenting with markers and came up with this fast, simple solution. After quickly applying a marker (Angela uses permanent, alcohol-based Faber-Castell markers) in a small area on a semiglossy or glossy photo, Angela rubs the area immediately before it dries with a soft cloth or lint-free paper towel to smooth out streaks. This gives the finish a subtle, matte look. Angela also uses a colorless blender marker to remove excess color, clean up areas, and add highlights.

Angela finds that pastel colors look best on photos, but notes that darker colors often end up several shades lighter after application. "It takes practice to learn which colors work best for you," Angela observes. "Some dark colors simply dry too fast to avoid streaking. However, there are plenty of colors which work beautifully and are simple to work with."

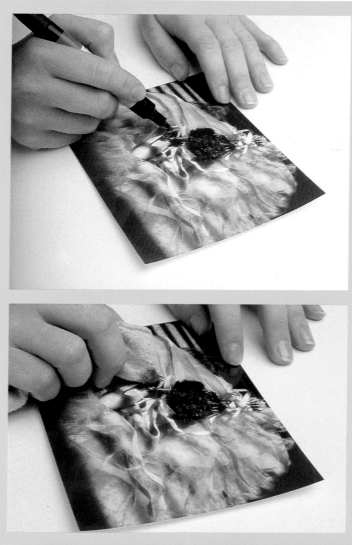

Step 1 Using a permanent Faber-Castell marker, apply color quickly in a small area. For best results, photos should have a semiglossy or glossy finish. Test before using on a matte finish.

Step 2 Rub the area with a soft cloth or lint-free paper towel before the color has a chance to dry. This smoothes out streaks and gives the color a soft, matte appearance. A colorless blender marker can also be used to remove unwanted color or to add highlights. Repeat these two basic steps until all desired areas are tinted.

Step 3 Adding color to a photo can greatly enhance its subject matter. Note how the pastel colors enhance the texture of the romantic ribbons flowing over the gauzy tulle.

**James M. Effler and
David Miller**

Airbrush Illustrators
A.I.R. Studio
Cincinnati, Ohio

When you're transferring a fairly simple drawing to a board for an airbrush illustration, experts James Effler and David Miller have found that the lead-pickup technique can really be a time-saver. But it's only effective under certain conditions: when your images have hard edges and when there aren't too many shapes to be cut out and repositioned.

Draw your image on tracing paper with a lead pencil. After taping the sketch to your final illustration board, position a piece of frisket over the entire drawing and burnish over all the lines. The adhesive side of the frisket will pick up some of the graphite from the pencil drawing. In record time you're ready to cut and spray.

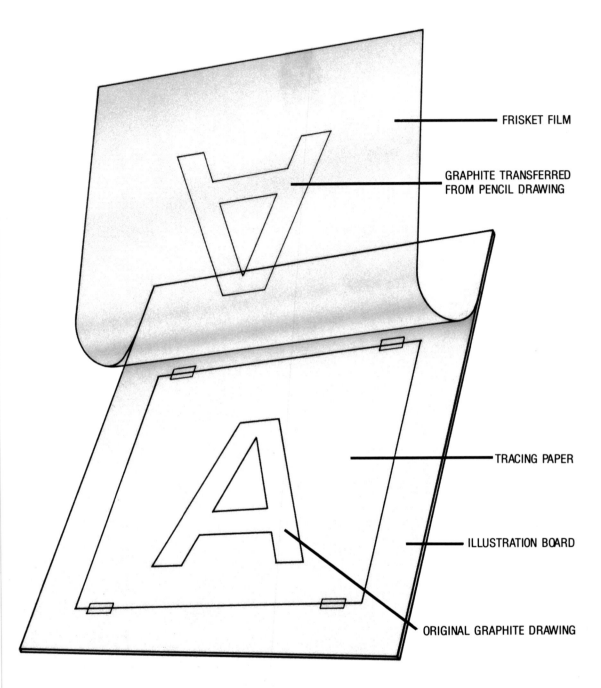

FRISKET FILM

GRAPHITE TRANSFERRED
FROM PENCIL DRAWING

TRACING PAPER

ILLUSTRATION BOARD

ORIGINAL GRAPHITE DRAWING

Begin by drawing your image on tracing paper with an H or 2H pencil. Make sure your lines are precise so you'll know exactly where to cut. Tape your pencil drawing to your final illustration board, which should be larger than the drawing on all sides.

Cover the entire drawing with a piece of frisket that overlaps it generously on at least one side.

That side will be used later as a hinge. Tape the frisket in place.

Now you're ready to burnish; be sure to apply enough pressure so the adhesive side of the frisket picks up some of the graphite. Pull the frisket up just enough to remove the original drawing, while leaving one side of the frisket hinged to the board. Now smooth the frisket back down on the board.

You've saved time transferring the drawing this way rather than by the usual carbon method, and you're now ready to cut.

Robert Hudnall

Graphic Designer
Lubbock, Texas

The photocopier has quickly become one of the graphic designer's most versatile design tools. In fact, a photocopier seems virtually indispensable when you consider the multitude of time-saving uses that designers describe in this book.

One shortcut is Robert Hudnall's technique of transferring an image to a frisket. After making a light photocopy, he covers it with frisket and burnishes well. Robert notes that this works best when the frisket is high-tack. The toner on the photocopy adheres to the frisket, and even complicated shapes show up clearly. Now you're ready to cut and spray in less than half the usual time.

Step 1   Make a light photocopy of your artwork. "All photocopiers are not alike," observes Robert, "so you may have to experiment. Generally, you'll get the best results with light copies." (Note that Robert did make a light photocopy, but because he was afraid that it wouldn't show up enough in this illustration, he retouched it with black ink!)

Step 2   Cover the photocopy with high-tack frisket and burnish well. Lift up a corner of the frisket to check the image transfer. The image will be light in most cases, but even complicated shapes should show up clearly. If some areas are uneven, you can always burnish the frisket a second time.

Tape the frisket to your board and cut and spray as you normally would. The frisket may not be quite as tacky as usual. This isn't a problem, but it is a good idea to burnish all cut edges firmly to avoid underspraying.

Step 3   Here is the airbrush work, shown superimposed over the photocopy of the image.

**James M. Effler and
David Miller**

Airbrush Illustrators
A.I.R. Studio
Cincinnati, Ohio

Textures in airbrush? That may seem as absurd as oil in water to you, but master airbrush illustrators James Effler and David Miller can show you how to extend the range of items you can render using texture. In addition to basic stippling, dry transfer, and liquid frisket techniques, there are four other ways of giving smooth, slick, or metallic surfaces more exciting, realistic dimensions. Dry-brushing, erasing, working with different masking materials, and using colored pencils will be described here.

Dry-brushing helps you create fine texture for such items as hair, fur, wood grain, and grass.

You do it by varying the amount of paint, strokes of your brush, and colors. After spraying a layer of airbrushed color, take a dry brush (select the size that's appropriate to the effect you want to simulate) and load it lightly (say, on one-eighth of the brush's tip) with water-color or gouache. Practice stroking with the brush until you achieve the effect you want—sometimes you have to press the brush down to the ferrule and twirl it slightly. Once you're satisfied, you're ready to apply strokes to your illustration. Always make sure to move light, fast strokes in the direction in which the object grows in nature. Also, it's good to make practice strokes each time you apply paint to the illustration. Repeat this as many times as needed to create

the effect you want.

Erasing is often the best way to add highlights, contours, or modeling to your illustration. You can produce a cleaner color by erasing than you can by spraying a light color over a darker one; spraying white may even muddy or dull darker colors instead of achieving the effect you want. Erasing freehand with either a hard or soft eraser produces a softer look than erasing through an acetate mask.

Innovative masking materials are helpful when you need to create a very specific texture—such as fabric, window screening, or any porous material. After spraying a base layer of color, you simply secure a mask of the material over the particular area, fix the base with a light coat of spray adhe-

sive to prevent underspraying, and spray a darker color through the mask. Be sure to wipe away any residue from the adhesive with Bestine solvent.

Colored pencils can help you simulate such effects as hair, asphalt, rough wood grain, and grass, which may be difficult or impossible to produce with the airbrush or a sable brush. One caution is that, unless blended with a cotton swab, hardlined colored pencil over airbrush may appear out of place when the artwork is photographed or separated for printing, so you might want to practice with colored pencils before applying them in a final illustration. If you decide to use colored pencils, be sure to do so as the last step in your illustration.

DRY-BRUSHING

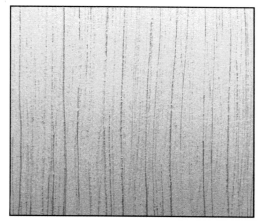

Dry-brushing lets you simulate a subtle wood grain effect.

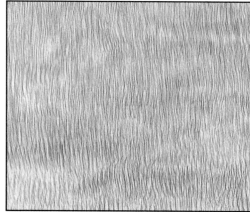
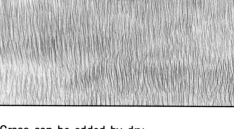

Grass can be added by drybrushing a darker color over a green base coat.

Adding graded darker gray over a silver base coat produces the look of aluminum.

COLORED PENCIL

Use the side of a pencil to create the rough texture of asphalt.

If you want to bring out the roughness of wood grain, you can add it with three different tones of colored pencil.

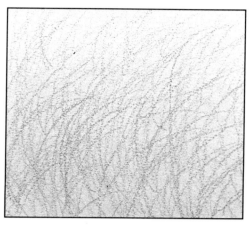

Working with a number of colored pencils helps convey the effect of blowing grass.

MASKING

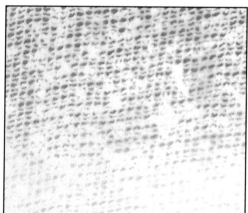

This is the result of using gauze as a mask. You could never create this precise, unusual effect any other way.

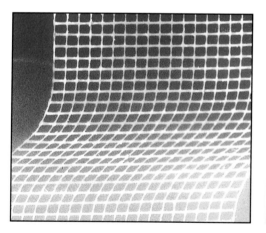

Window screening produces a grid pattern. Note that you can render this with all lines parallel by laying the screening on the board or with the lines curved, as shown here, by curving the screening before you spray.

ERASING

Working slowly with a kneaded or soft gum eraser lets you create softer, more subtle effects than if you used a hard rubber or ink eraser.

Jim Connelly

Illustrator
Airow Studio
Wyoming, Michigan

With over 15 years experience, Jim Connelly is an accomplished airbrush illustrator. But even he admits that "airbrush work is often so smooth it's boring." To add tension and interest to his work, Jim began experimenting. What he discovered was a way to create varied, textured backgrounds not usually seen in airbrush work.

Jim's secret ingredient is Fantastik, the common household cleaner. He sprays it on a board that has been airbrushed with two layers of acrylic paint (the first layer is coated with the fixative Krylon) and then blots the wet surface with paper towel, plastic wrap, or other materials to create varied effects. The cleaner dissolves some of the top layer of paint, allowing the lower layer to show through in a random pattern, and the blotting material creates additional texture.

The effects you can achieve with different combinations of acrylic colors—the technique doesn't work with watercolor or gouache—and ways of applying and blotting the cleaner make this an extremely versatile, exciting technique. "Like other methods of painting, it takes practice to learn to control the media. Have fun experimenting," encourages Jim.

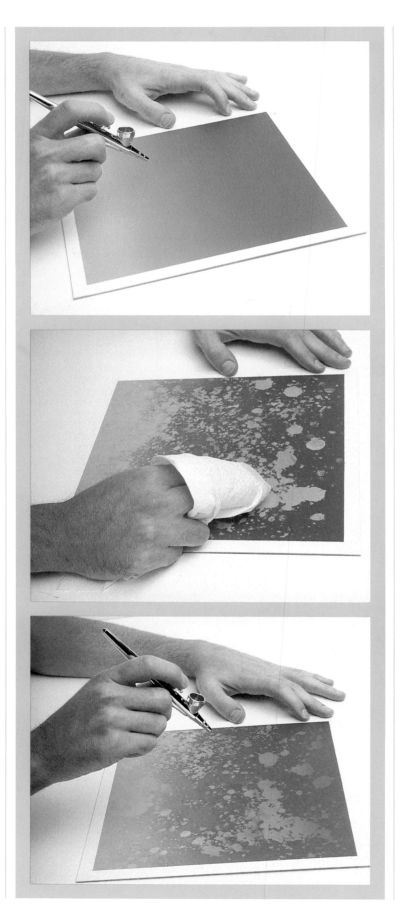

Step 1 Jim begins by airbrushing a layer of light blue acrylic on the board and then covers it with a coat of Krylon fixative. Then he applies dark blue acrylic, carefully gradating the dark blue into the light.

Step 2 Now he sprays the entire board with Fantastik directly from a bottle. Quickly, before the drops dry, he blots them with a paper towel, creating a unique pattern, and then he lets the board dry.

Step 3 To give the background a sophisticated finish, Jim sprays a second light gradation of dark blue acrylic.

Step 4 Note how the unusual background treatment adds drama to the final illustration. Jim did the horse's head using standard airbrush techniques, involving a number of friskets. He painted finishing touches, such as the scrolling on the saddle, by hand with acrylic paint.

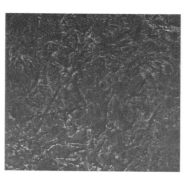  

To create this mottled background treatment, Jim covers the board with a layer of dark gray acrylic and gives it a coating of Krylon fixative. He covers that with a coat of medium gray acrylic, spraying evenly. Then he sprays Fantastik through an airbrush for a thorough application until the board is quite wet.

Wadding up ordinary bond typing paper, he presses it on the surface. After letting the board dry, he gives it another coating of Krylon. Then he applies an even coat of sepia acrylic, again sprays the board with Fantastik, and blots it with crumpled paper.

Jim begins this pattern by coating the board with Krylon and applying an even coat of magenta. Then he sprays Fantastik through an airbrush until the entire board is very wet. Taking a piece of plastic wrap about the size of the background and wadding it up, Jim presses it against the board and pulls it up, carefully going over the entire board, before he lets it dry.

After applying another coat of Krylon, he sprays the board with an even coat of red acrylic. Jim completes the background by applying another layer of Fantastik and modifying the pattern with more plastic wrap.

This texture is created after two layers of acrylic—tan coated with Krylon and dark brown sprayed evenly—are covered with a light layer of Fantastik sprayed through an airbrush. Again, the illustrator achieves the grainy effect by blotting the Fantastik with a wad of bond paper.

Jim uses the same colors as in the last example but reverses them. Beginning with a coat of dark brown acrylic covered with Krylon, he then applies an even layer of tan. After using an airbrush to spray the board with a light layer of Fantastik, he wads up bond paper and presses it over the entire board. To create the delicate, filmy texture, he adds a light coat of transparent brown acrylic.

This illustration was commissioned by the Radio Bible Class for a cassette they produced entitled "Overflowing Heart." Jim began by spraying a layer of beige acrylic over the illustration board. After it dried, he coated it with Krylon. Then he sprayed a light, even coat of sky blue over the board and followed that with a heavy coat of Fantastik, sprayed through the airbrush. He made sure that coat was heavy enough to create a wet look but not heavy enough to run.

Then Jim pressed a large piece of bond paper that had been wadded up into a ball into the wet board and then unwadded the paper and pressed it into the board again. Says Jim, "The wrinkles that were left in the paper are what created the unusual patterns." To complete the illustration, Jim rendered the red brush stroke in airbrush with a dry-brush technique and the water by airbrushing transparent acrylic and erasing the highlights with an ink eraser.

Used with permission of Jim Connelly.

This lively illustration ran in the September 1988 issue of Grand Rapids' *On the Town* magazine. Here's how Jim did the background: He sprayed the top with yellow acrylic and faded violet into magenta at the bottom, covering the board with a clear coat of matte-finish Krylon.

Then he gave the board a light coat of white, followed by a wet coat of Fantastik, sprayed with the airbrush. Over the wet board, Jim laid crumpled plastic wrap, patted it down, and pulled it up carefully. To subdue the contrast, he finished the background with a series of light layers of transparent yellow, magenta, and violet.

Mark Mealy

Designer
Greenwell Goetz Architects
Washington, D.C.

There's nothing new about using masks in airbrush work. What makes designer Mark Mealy's masking technique unusual is the material he uses: Post-it Notes. These adhesive sheets, which come in a variety of sizes, are particularly suited to defining hard edges, or they can be cut or torn into one-of-a-kind shapes.

Mark began experimenting with the notes to save time on his job—he does airbrush renderings for a Washington, D.C., architectural firm. "Basically, the technique harnesses the light-tack adhesive of the Post-it to mask uncomplicated shapes for airbrush," Mark states. "They save time and money because they eliminate cutting more expensive frisket paper, and they can be reused several times before losing adhesion."

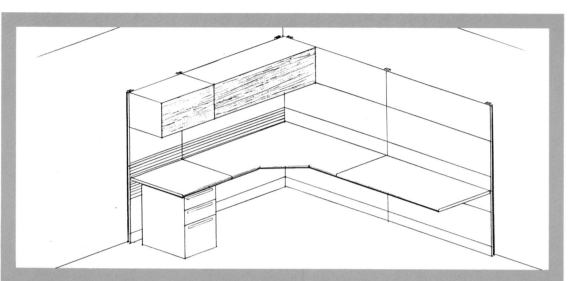

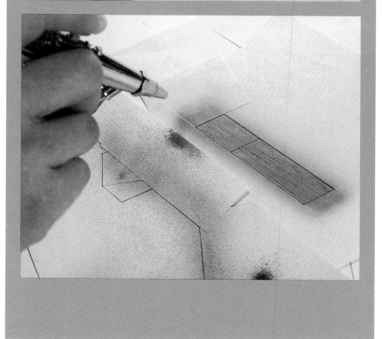

Step 1 Here is an orthographic drawing of an office area Mark wants to airbrush.

Step 2 First, he applies a gray tone to the middle area. Note how he has used a combination of large and small Post-it Notes.

Step 3 Here the designer has cut the notes to isolate two brown areas.

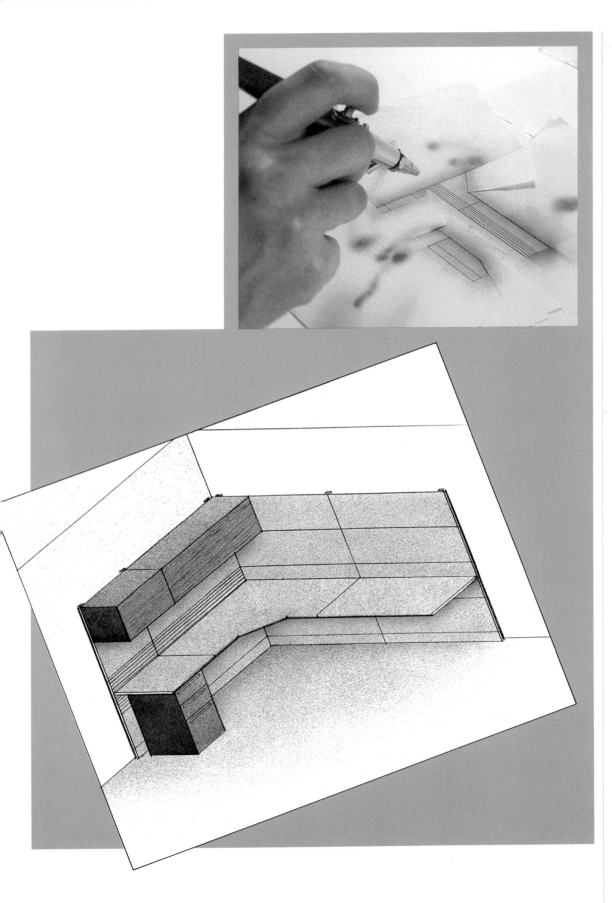

Step 4 Precise cutting is required to mask off tiny areas of the blue background. But the time that took was much less than if the designer had cut a conventional mask.

Step 5 To complete the rendering, Mark airbrushes the top of the cabinet, the file drawers, and the blue background on the right.

In this airbrush project, Mark is designing a company logo. Rather than use new Post-it Notes, Mark decided to reuse some from an earlier job. (Note several colors on the Post-its that were not used in this project.) Being able to reuse these handy sheets helps you save both time and money.

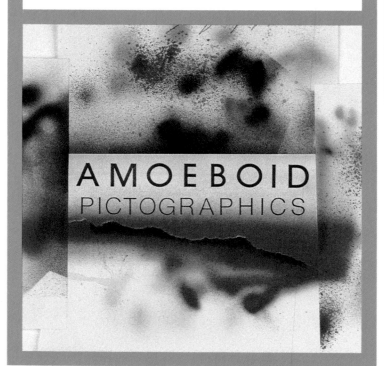

Step 1 Mark wants to design a logo for this company.

Step 2 Reusing notes he had used on an earlier job, the designer masks off the area he wants to airbrush. He selects magenta and blue for his color scheme.

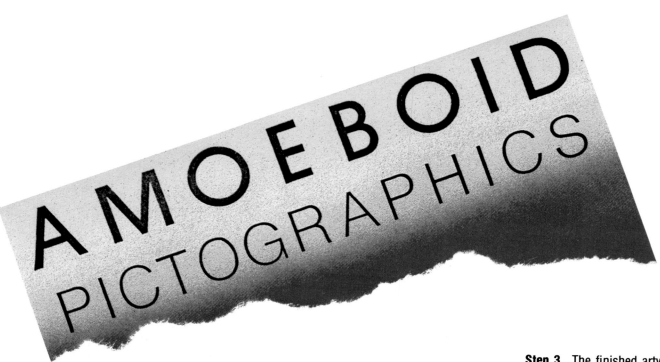

Step 3 The finished artwork is a good example of the unique effect created with a torn mask.

John E. Thies

Senior Graphic Designer
AT&T Bell Laboratories
Art Studio
Reading, Pennsylvania

"Artists have perfected the airbrushed 'star burst' on countless pieces of art," observes John E. Thies, whose job as senior designer at AT&T Bell Labs Art Studio involves rendering light-emitting products. "After years of 'painting in' these light sources, I now have a process that makes artwork 'jump' off the photo because it incorporates a real star burst using real light. The secret works best," John advises, "when the two-dimensional artwork is showing light or a reflected light source—stars, bursts, light bulbs, fiberoptics, chrome, etc."

With the aid of AT&T photographer Chuck Russo, John spent 27 hours experimenting with this technique before perfecting it. While executing this secret requires a highly sophisticated photo lab and custom printing, it does offer to the adventurous graphic artist with photographic insight a real alternative to airbrushing.

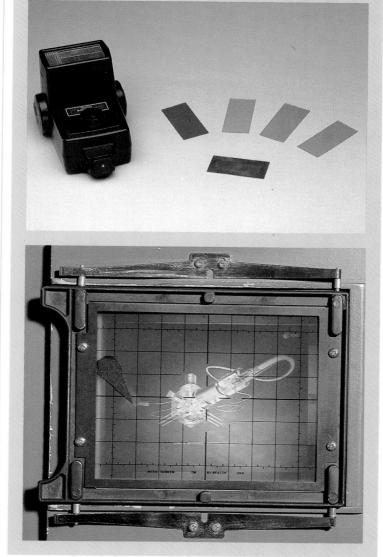

Step 1 This shows the finished artwork before the star-burst effect is added to the end of the connector on the left side of the photograph. The challenge is to align the real light at precisely the right spot on the connector to create the star burst.

Step 2 This setup shows (clockwise from top left) the Vivitar 283 strobe, filters, and the metal plate with a 1/10,000-inch aperture through which the strobe is fired for the second exposure. The filters are needed to balance strobe to tungsten light, with the magenta filter used to match the color of the laser fiber output.

Step 3 Now you're ready to proceed with the technique. Mount the artwork. Set up a 4"×5" view camera opposite it so that the artwork image fills the ground glass, as you can see in this photograph. Shoot the artwork with polarized light. Now place an arrow cut from black tape on the camera's ground glass to indicate the precise location where the star burst is to appear on the finished negative or transparency.

Step 4 Locate a bright light behind the camera and open the camera aperture and shutter. This projects the arrow onto the artwork; the arrow must remain on the ground glass until all shooting is completed. "It is extremely critical," John cautions, "that the camera and artwork remain stationary throughout the process. The slightest movement of either will cause misalignment of the star burst on the artwork."

Step 5 Use a white card to help you position the projected arrow on the artwork. Now mount on your lens the Tiffen star burst filter equipped with a custom-rotating mount (optional) and 4mm grids. The position of the filter grids determines at what angle the rays of the burst will travel.

You may want to experiment with Polaroid film on this step to determine the correct f-stop and to get the effect you want. John notes, "It's impossible to tell you which f-stop to use—it depends entirely on your artwork and the effect you want to create. In this instance, f16 was used."

Step 6 With the camera aperture and shutter open, move the strobe light, which faces *into* the lens, into final alignment with the projected image of the arrow. "Attaching the strobe light to a tripod will facilitate the alignment, allowing precise positioning," John advises. "Also, the distance of the strobe to the camera determines the size of the star burst." The flash unit is shown here, mounted on a tripod, with the metal plate with the 1/10,000-inch aperture taped on the flash window.

Close and cock the shutter and insert the film holder with the same piece of film exposed in Step 3. Now, in total darkness, fire the strobe into the camera.

Step 7 In the finished artwork the star burst seems to jump off the photo, adding excitement and tension to the final piece.

All photographs and studio setups by Chuck Russo.

Mark Riedy

Airbrush Illustrator
Dayton, Ohio

Many illustrators think of airbrushing only solid, opaque objects. But it's good to be versatile. Airbrush illustrator Mark Riedy has come up with an easy method for creating transparent objects like the ice cubes shown here. What makes ice seem complicated is that it acts like an irregular lens, distorting shapes beyond recognition. That means you have to create a variety of focuses, some very sharp and others very diffuse. The trick is to give the shifting shapes and colors a shimmering yet solid look and feel. Ice is colorless, but blues are traditionally used to convey it.

Greg LaFever worked in conjunction with Mark on this illustration.

Step 1 Although you think of ice as clear and transparent, its irregular surfaces are really made up of a minute variety of shapes, colors, and subtle details. Begin by outlining the ice cubes on your illustration board with a black technical pen; then fill in some areas to show mass and shape.

Step 2 Cover the illustration with a sheet of frisket, and cut out the areas you want to be blue—the top of the background and the reflections in each cube. Fill your airbrush with slate blue dye mixed with two drops of jungle green. After you've sprayed evenly in both areas, add a little black for density. Replace the frisket.

Step 3 Now you're ready to add more subtle detail on the top, sides, and face of the cubes. Determine which irregular shapes you want to be gray and cut and remove the frisket in those areas. Be sure to leave white edges between some of the gray and black shapes. This helps create the shimmering quality inherent in ice. Spray diluted black dye, holding the airbrush very close to the surface. Replace the frisket.

Step 4 Cut and remove the frisket from the entire front of the ice cubes. Decide which middle areas to soften and cut masks for them. Mix a few drops of diluted black with jungle green to gray the color. Spray the masked areas, making sure to hold the masks slightly above the painted surfaces to soften the edges. Remove the masks and the entire frisket.

Step 5 To add further overall refinement, place a new piece of frisket over the illustration. Cut out shapes on the top and face of each cube and spray a light coat of gray-green (from Step 4) that has been diluted with water. This tone will help emphasize the highlights. Replace the frisket.

Step 6 Now it's time to do the dark lower areas on the face of each cube; this darkening results from the tabletop reflecting through the ice. Cut and remove the frisket and spray diluted black dye freehand. Replace the frisket.

Step 7 To add dimension to the tabletop, cut and remove the frisket around the ice cubes. Hold the airbrush 3 to 4 inches away from the illustration as you spray a light, even gray tone. Move the airbrush closer to darken some odd-shaped areas under the cubes. Now clean the airbrush and, using slate blue dye, add a light blue tint to the irregular highlights on the table under the cubes. Remove all the frisket.

Step 8 To increase the sense of solidity at the bottom of the cubes, introduce wavy lines with Prussian blue, dark green, and black colored pencils. Now load a small sable brush with opaque white and add highlights. At last, you're ready for the final step: creating white reflections on the top and face of the cubes to make some shapes look like they're under the surface. After you tear a paper mask and spray diluted opaque white in some areas, your irregular, shimmering ice cubes are complete.

Mark Riedy

Airbrush Illustrator
Dayton, Ohio

Splashing paint is not easy to illustrate in any medium. Unless you're endowed with your own darkroom, a comfortable deadline, and a fat budget, doing your own photography may pose too many obstacles, making airbrush a more realistic option. Yet airbrushing an opaque liquid in motion is hardly a snap, even though master airbrush illustrator Mark Reidy makes it look that way.

One of the secrets of his success is researching the subject thoroughly. You should not only study what photo references you can find, but also take the time to observe liquid as it is being poured, as it splashes, and as it rests on a flat surface. Then after you've accurately captured the shape of the paint in a sketch, you can render it as though it were a solid mass of reflective plastic, adding a rich variety of interesting highlights and shadows.

Greg LaFever worked in conjunction with Mark on this illustration.

Step 1   After you've completed your sketch, begin by rendering the paint cans. (Instructions are for the right-hand can; work on the left one simultaneously.) Place a sheet of frisket on the top half of the illustration and cut out the paint cans. Load your airbrush with equal parts of slate blue and black dye. Now, working from the outside of the rim toward the center, remove the frisket from around the thin outer rim. Spray carefully along one edge, making sure to hold the airbrush very close to the illustration's sur-

face. Replace the frisket. Skip the next circle of white—this helps create the rounded-looking, reflective surface—and remove the next circle of frisket. This time, apply less tone. Gradating the tone also helps create the cylindrical curve of the can.

Continue working inward, circle by circle, until you have completed the dark interior of the can. Now, remove all the frisket from the rim and add a hint of reflected color by spraying it with a light layer of cerulean blue. Replace the frisket.

Now it's time to work on the can's exterior surface. Begin by removing the frisket and mixing pansy dye with two drops of slate blue and one drop of black until the color cup is three-quarters full. Spray the exterior, making sure to gradate the tone and add the shadow cast by the rim. Remove all the frisket, and add dark lines to define some edges with a small sable brush and black dye. To finish the cans, add soft white highlights with opaque white.

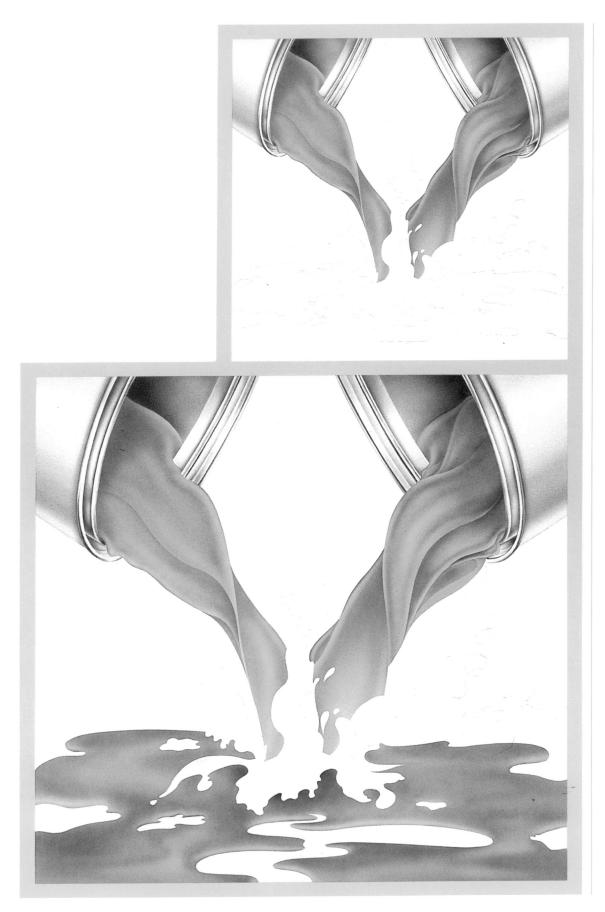

Step 2 Now you're ready to start on the paint. Cover the entire board with frisket, and load the airbrush with moss green. Cut along all the lines of the pouring paint, making sure to create different shapes within it for streams. Now section by section, remove the frisket and spray the subtle shadings within each shape freehand. Note how they overlap and fold into each other. Don't forget to add highlights and shadows.

Step 3 Now it's time to do the paint resting on the lower surface. Cut along all the lines and remove the frisket. Spray it a medium coat of moss green. Because a liquid's properties give it thickness as it rests on a flat surface, you need to create this look. Add subtle, soft-edged darks by spraying freehand along the edges and across the surface. The area under the splash should be especially dark to help create the illusion of three-dimensionality in the splash. Replace the frisket.

Step 4 Cut along all the lines of the splash. What you need to remember here is that the splash is essentially a random scattering of paint whose shapes are more rounded than those on the flat surface. Spray each area separately. To help you create the shadows and highlights within the rounded shapes, visualize a constant light source. When you're finished, remove all the frisket.

Step 5 Now you're ready to add white highlights along some edges to give the paint a glossy look. Place an acetate mask over the entire illustration, cut out all the areas you've designated for thin white highlights, and position the mask slightly above the illustration surface to soften the images. Spray several thin coats of diluted opaque white. To add additional variations, fill in some areas with a grass green colored pencil, always keeping your light source in mind.

Step 6 To add final details, mask the lower flat surface and cut out the areas of white around the paint. Spray light shadows freehand with diluted black dye to increase the three-dimensionality of the resting paint. Your illustration of splashing paint is now complete.

Lesley Schiff

Artist
New York, New York

Artist Lesley Schiff has found a way to paint with light. Her high-tech secret requires a Canon color laser photocopier. "I think one of the most exciting things about the color photocopier is that the light is in the tool," explains Lesley, who studied classical and modern painting at the Art Institute of Chicago before becoming a commercial and fine artist. "I find it a highly refined instrument, and I'm particularly attracted by the clear, sharp, but soft color quality." Another plus, says Lesley, is that "it goes as fast as your mind goes and the result is instantaneous. It combines photography and painting—but my intention is to make a painting, not a photograph."

After endless experimentation at a color photocopy shop in the early 1980s, Lesley's work came to Canon's attention, and now she works as a technical consultant on the laser photocopier. The machine offers an amazing range of technical possibilities—such as softening or sharpening an image, color conversion, and a zoom feature that reduces and enlarges in a range of 50 to 400 percent in 1 percent increments. It's the only color photocopier to include black in addition to magenta, yellow, and cyan toner.

· Lesley incorporated elements from her extensive prop closet in the album cover for the Ban-gles rock group shown here. To achieve a shimmering effect, she moved a sheet of white paper over the photo and the props during the machine's color passes.

Step 1   To create an album cover for the Bangles rock group, Lesley composes the image on the glass surface of the Canon color laser photocopier. She assembles ferns, a charm bracelet, and other trinkets around a black-and-white photograph of the group.

Step 2   Here is the first rough shot of Lesley's arrangement. She studies it carefully, evaluating its composition, color, and proportions.

Step 3   Lesley finds the composition too loose and skimpy, so she adds more fern leaves and uses the zoom feature to enlarge the photo. Now she covers the composition with a sheet of white paper to contain the light that the machine projects onto the image. Note that Lesley also varied the background color here, making it more vivid.

Step 4 Still not satisfied with the background color, the artist creates a more intense, focused range of purples, blues, and oranges by manipulating the sheet of white paper during the machine's four color passes under the image. Note that Lesley has also zoomed the photograph down to a more appropriate size.

Step 5 After making final adjustments in the composition, Lesley "prints" this final illustration, which will be stripped into the album cover mechanical.

Step 6 Lesley's unique artwork captured the rock group's image so well on this album cover that, in addition to creating the rest of the group's packaging for related items produced by CBS Records, she was asked to do the sets for the Bangles' live stage show.

Peter Kuper

Illustrator and Cartoonist
New York, New York

How do you design a jacket illustration for a book of comic strips that are about the mind-blowing complexities of living in New York City? That's the challenge illustrator Peter Kuper gave himself with his book *New York, New York*. But it wasn't as easy as it looks here. Peter's design went through three versions before it reflected the book's contents to his satisfaction. "I wanted to sum up the book with one image that expressed its content in as concise a way as possible," notes Peter, "but at the same time not throw out subtlety so that the viewer would be able to look at it more than once."

When the brainstorm for the final jacket finally hit, Peter had already approved color separations for the second jacket design. He told his editor at Fantagraphic Books that he would send a revised final layout that afternoon by express delivery. Using a combination of cartooning and collage, and assisted by a home photocopier and an extensive picture file, Peter completed a comp for this dynamic illustration in a hectic four hours.

Step 1   One feature of Peter's design that remained constant in all three versions of the book jacket is his treatment of the title. He wanted to juxtapose the classic type from the *New York Times* logo with graffiti typography to capture the city's contrasts. Here Peter cuts out his specially designed graffiti letters with an X-Acto knife to make a stencil for the title.

Step 2   The artist spray paints the lettering in black Krylon on white bond paper.

Step 3   Peeling off the stencil, Peter decides the lettering needs a rougher feel to convey the tensions of city living, so he goes over the letters again with a toothbrush, ink, and white correction fluid.

Step 4 Peter has the two logos and his name shot in a direct negative stat while preparing the rest of the layout. Note how many different typefaces Peter considered before picking the one for his name.

Step 5 Peter begins the illustration by sketching his favorite character, who has evolved over a number of years into an Everyman figure—Charlie Chaplin mixed with Woody Allen, with a little Harold Lloyd thrown in for good measure. Here Peter traces the face in ink with a crow quill pen.

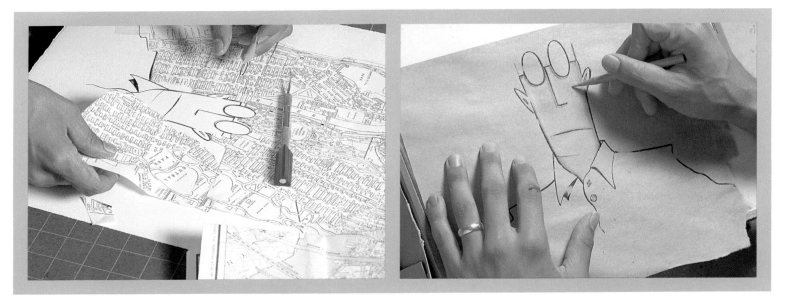

Step 6 For the background, he photocopies a map of New York City and rips it up, rearranging the pieces around the head with an X-Acto knife and tape. He uses this black-and-white layout as a template for Steps 10 and 11.

Step 7 Then the artist returns to the figure. He photocopies the face twice: on a piece of brown paper bag and on a sheet of white paper. Then he photocopies the figure on a sheet of blue Color-Aid paper. Here he adds color to the face with Prismacolor pencils.

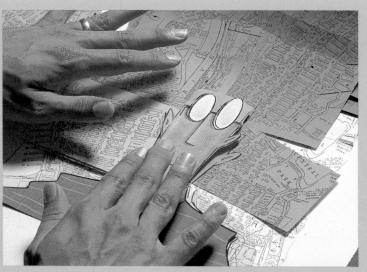

Step 8 For greater refinement of the figure, Peter draws a pattern on the blue shirt with Prismacolor pencils. To add white eyeglasses to the figure, Peter highlights them first on the white photocopy with a blue Prismacolor pencil and then cuts them out and pastes them on the face.

Step 9 Now the artist photocopies parts of the map on different colored sheets of Color-Aid paper. After ripping off sections of the map, Peter positions them around the character.

Step 10 Peter applies glue to all the elements before positioning them on 140-lb hot-press watercolor paper.

Step 11 Now Peter's ready to add the images of buildings that personify the city. So he hunts through his files for clippings. After cutting the pictures out with an X-Acto knife, including the Empire State Building shown here, Peter begins positioning them around the figure's head.

Step 12 But Peter isn't satisfied. He decides that the face needs to pop out more from the background, so he adds a shadow on the right by cutting out a section of the map photocopied on purple paper. He completes the illustration by putting his signature in a vertical orange strip.

Step 13 ''New York just blows his mind'' is Peter's comment on the final illustration.

PETER KUPER'S
New York
NEW YORK

FANTAGRAPHICS BOOKS

Linda Bourke

Freelance Illustrator
Teacher, Massachusetts
College of Art
Cambridge, Massachusetts

One day illustrator Linda Bourke made a mistake while she was copying a sketch. She accidentally twisted it as the photocopier's light moved under the image. "The resulting copy provided a new 'slant' that I liked so much I decided to use it for the finished illustration," says Linda. Ever since, she has been experimenting with a photocopier to create elongated, stretched, twisted, or distorted effects. Enlarging the image at the same time adds to the variety of possible effects.

It helps if the image is fairly simple, notes Linda. The only technical requirements are that the light in the photocopier move under the image and that you manipulate the image slowly. "I've used this secret several times for both drawing and typographic solutions," admits Linda, "and I still get great surprises!"

For additional ways to take advantage of this technique, note Mark Allison's secret, showing how charcoal images produced on both bond and charcoal paper are affected by photocopying (Secret 52, Quick, Low-Cost Conversions).

Here is a conventional copy of Linda's original pencil drawing.

Slanting the image to the left produced this variation.

A combination of both a right and left motion led to this distorted effect (far left).

Dragging the image diagonally over the light generated this exaggerated image (left).

This copy (below) was created by slowly twisting the image to the right at a sharp angle.

Here Linda shows what she was able to achieve by manipulating typography on a photocopier. Even though you may need to touch up parts of the letters, it's time well spent. A little experimentation at the photocopier can provide highly original results.

Step 1 The press-down type Linda picked for this example is Simplex Bold.

Step 2 On this page you can see five different kinds of distortion that Linda achieved by manipulating the type in different directions on the photocopier.

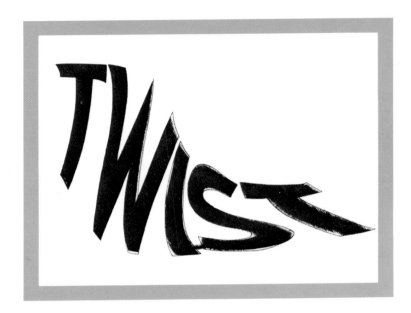

Step 3 Linda touched up the distorted type with a technical pen so that all the edges are clean and crisp.

Step 4 Distorted type can lend a unique, high-tech character to your designs, as illustrated by the two examples above.

Howard F. Bradybaugh

Technical Illustrator
Museum Graphics
Rush, New York

Some designers welcome every opportunity to do fine-line ink drawings. Others don't really enjoy picking up a pen. No matter where you are along that spectrum, the high-tech method adapted by technical illustrator Howard Bradybaugh will give you precise, clean ink drawings every time. There are no smudged guidelines, messy erasures, or heavily worked backgrounds because—here's the secret—you're not really drawing on the final paper or board. Instead, you copy your original pencil drawing on a photocopier fitted with an interchangeable blue development system. Then you simply ink over the light blue lines. Color overlays can always be added to the final mechanical.

Howard perfected this technique while working for eight years on a series of maps of world airmail routes for a five-volume set of catalogs. "The blue line method was extremely useful in this project," he explains, "as there were hundreds of revisions and additions to the original pencil layouts which also had to be retained for updating future editions."

Being able to file your original pencil drawing is an added advantage of this technique. Another is that you can always reverse, enlarge, or reduce the image—and your corresponding drawing—on the photocopier. An investment of approximately $300 for the blue developer system seems reasonable when you consider the time and effort you can save with this surefire illustration method.

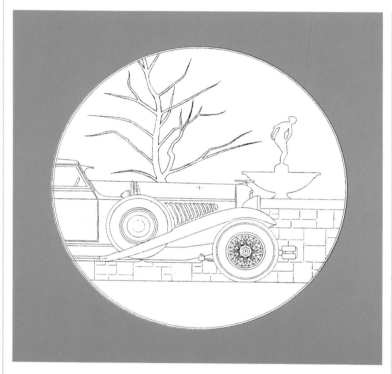

Step 1 One of Howard's favorite, long-standing personal projects is drawing antique automobiles. This drawing of a 1932 Duesenberg was done on tracing paper, including all final revisions. The illustrator notes that lines should be thin, sharp, and consistently dark enough for a photocopier lens to pick them up.

Step 2 After inserting the interchangeable blue developing system into the photocopier, set the copy contrast control for a lighter-than-normal printout. Make test copies on regular paper to achieve the shade of light blue that is just dark enough for you to see as you ink over the lines. Then position the pencil drawing on the photocopier so that it will fall exactly where you wish on the paper. Next, hand-feed a single sheet of heavier paper, such as 2- or 3-ply bristol board, through the machine.

Step 3 Before you begin inking, it's best to rub down the blue image lightly with pounce or a Pink Pearl eraser. That ensures better adherence of the ink and also helps lighten the blue image even more for easier coverage. You can also use an electric eraser at any time during the inking process to eliminate reference points, unwanted blue lines, or smudges picked up by the photocopier.

Step 4 Shading, cross-hatching, or final decorative touches can be added once the basic drawing is finished. Note that Howard added detail in the auto roof and body, tire, and background wall.

1932 Duesenberg

Randall Rayon

Illustrator
New York, New York

"I've always approached art with a very detailed look," says illustrator Randall Rayon, describing how he works with colored pencils. A successful fashion illustrator who landed a job with Neiman-Marcus fresh out of college, Randall goes on to explain: "The total airbrush look doesn't appeal to me because it seems too manufactured, too slick. The first thing I see is the technique, not the image. Even though my work looks polished, I like the richness of texture and the three-dimensional quality I'm able to achieve with colored pencils and watercolor washes."

Because Randall insists on precision, he admits that his colored pencil technique requires hours of painstaking concentration as he builds up many fine layers of color. Yet he acknowledges the special opportunities the medium offers. "I like the challenge of combining two- and three-dimensional elements in one drawing. The contrast interests me. My goal is *not* to make a drawing that looks like a photograph."

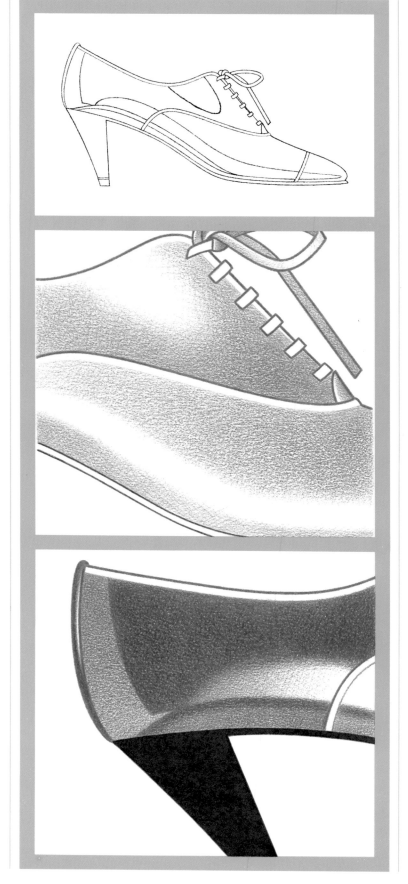

Step 1 Randall does a moderately detailed line drawing, working out the composition of images on tracing paper. Then he transfers the sketch to a slightly textured illustration paper.

Step 2 Starting with the darkest areas, Randall begins lightly laying in tones by crosshatching in various directions with a colored pencil of medium hardness—in this case, a Berol Verithin brown. After establishing the tone, he outlines the shoe with an extremely hard pencil for a clean line.

Step 3 Randall builds up the darkest areas with many fine layers of colored pencil, making sure to incorporate areas of light and shadow for a three-dimensional effect. After outlining the heel and sole with a technical pen loaded with black ink, he fills in the heel with a dense black ink, giving those areas a contrasting two-dimensional effect.

Step 4 To complete the shoe, Randall softens the edges of the dark tones with feathering pencil strokes to bleed them into the lighter areas. Using a Rapidograph loaded with colored ink, Randall completes the stitching. To add a moderate highlight to the heel, Randall goes in lightly with a white colored pencil.

The shoe is just one of several elements in the final fashion illustration, which appeared in *Elle*'s Fall 1988 Accessory Report.

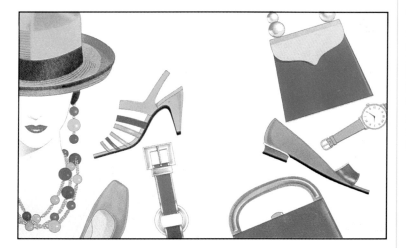

This fashion illustration, which ran in *Elle*'s Spring 1989 Accessory Report, provides another example of Randall Rayon's highly exact, yet textured work. Note that he incorporated three techniques here: colored pencil, colored pencil over Luma watercolor washes, and just Luma watercolor washes.

Sharon Watts

Illustrator
Brooklyn, New York

Tired of working with pen and ink? Looking for another, more exciting medium? That's what motivated illustrator Sharon Watts to begin experimenting with colored paper. "I was burned out after doing slick black-and-white illustrations for ten years," admits Sharon, "so I began fooling around with colored paper. Paper looks simple, yet it offers so many possibilities—color, texture, pattern, weight—just like fabric. Besides, it looks fresh. No one else is doing it. And my clients love it."

Sharon particularly appreciates the resistance paper offers. "I find the paper's personality ends up taking over. No matter how much I plan an illustration, the piece always evolves as I work with the paper. That makes working a challenge and a constant source of surprises."

Originally, Sharon did this illustration, highlighting a chance to win a trip to New Orleans, in black and white for a Macy's calendar advertisement that ran in the *New York Times*. She recreated the jazz scene in color especially for this book.

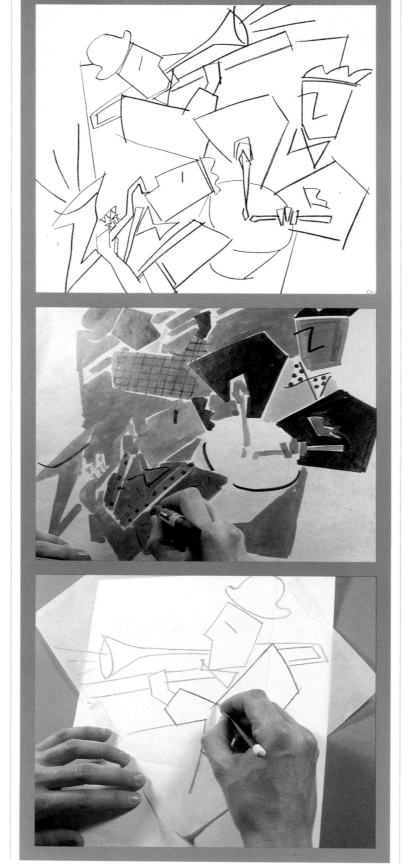

Step 1 Sharon does a pencil sketch on tracing paper, composing the general shapes that will become cut paper in the finished illustration. It usually takes Sharon several tries to get the design details worked out at this stage, though she notes that the illustration always evolves when the actual cutting and assembling of the paper takes place (see Step 4).

Step 2 Now Sharon does a color overlay on tracing paper using alcohol-based AD markers. After mapping out the general color scheme, she picks out the paper—"anything from Pantone sheets and Color-Aid to marbleized imports."

Step 3 Turning over the tight pencil rough (from Step 1), Sharon places it over the *back* of the paper she plans to cut. Then she goes over the shapes on the tracing paper with a hard pencil. This transfers the outlines to the colored paper and eliminates the need to erase pencil marks later.

Step 4 Now Sharon applies an even layer of one-coat rubber cement to the back of the colored paper, making sure to overlap her strokes for maximum coverage. After the glue dries, Sharon cuts out the shapes with an X-Acto knife. (By cutting the paper after gluing, Sharon prevents the glue from seeping over to the good side of the paper.)

After lightly transferring her composition onto a sheet of bristol or bond paper, Sharon is ready to paste the shapes in position. ''The one-coat cement allows for repositioning so that I can deviate from my original rough if I want to,'' notes Sharon. ''At this stage, unexpected details usually occur to me—things I couldn't have planned in Step 1. One of the things I like about this medium is that you can never predict the end result in its entirety.''

Step 5 After Sharon pastes all the shapes in her composition, she presses the illustration under a large book overnight before handing in the job.

This energetic illustration by Sharon Watts, which includes pastel and gouache details in addition to cut paper, originally appeared in the Shopping Guide of *New York Woman* magazine.

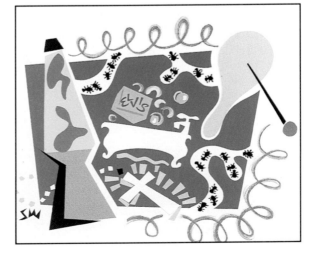

45   Experimenting with Unusual Tools

Lenore Simon

Artist and Printmaker
San Diego, California

Part of the challenge of being a graphic artist is discovering new ways to express ideas visually. So when an opportunity comes along that lets you create something new and exciting, it helps to have a few tricks up your sleeve. Artist Lenore Simon has several she's willing to share.

After spending nearly 20 years doing traditional intaglio printmaking, she won a grant and finally had time to try out new tools in her work: "found" objects, oil-based clay, rollers, x-rays, and plastic wrap are a few examples. "They allow for spontaneity as well as control over the finished piece," Lenore comments. "The methods are suitable for commercial applications as well as for fine art pieces. While I use water-based inks for their non-toxic qualities and easy clean-up, oil-based media may also be used as desired." Often she combines several techniques in each work.

Here, Lenore uses a "found" object. She takes a common household item—a small plastic basket that fruit and vegetables are sold in—and converts one side into a template.

Step 1 The artist places one side of the plastic basket on a sheet of scrap paper and inks it with a roller loaded with water-based printer's ink. She makes sure the ink is applied evenly and thoroughly.

Step 2 Picking up the template with her fingers, she carefully places it in position on her artwork and presses it against the paper with her hand. Slowly and deliberately she removes the template.

Step 3 The finished multimedia piece is entitled "Why Not"—an apt title, considering the number of "found" objects it contains and the unconventional approach used in creating it.

Lenore Simon

Artist and Printmaker
San Diego, California

"When dealing with an object that is too valuable to ink, flexible plastic wrap or small plastic bags can be placed on the form, that material can be inked, and the most detailed design can be offset on paper," states inventive artist Lenore Simon. "This method allows for transferring a complex design as observed and not in a mirror image. It's also effective because an artist can 'pull' shapes from three-dimensional surfaces." That's why Lenore used plastic wrap here to print part of a disassembled candlestick.

Step 1 The artist rolls water-based printer's ink on to a portion of a disassembled candlestick, making sure to cover it completely with an even layer of ink.

Step 2 Taking a sheet of plastic wrap, Lenore rubs it firmly over the inked candlestick to transfer the inked impression.

Step 3 Immediately, she presses the highly detailed impression onto her illustration board, rubbing it gently and thoroughly. She checks to make sure the transfer is complete before removing the plastic wrap template.

Step 4 Another in the series of *Symbols of My People* (see page 99) this multimedia work was produced using several of the methods described elsewhere. In addition to colored pencils, the artist used both the broad side and the edge of a roller.

Lenore Simon

Artist and Printmaker
San Diego, California

You may think of clay as something only kids play with, but artist Lenore Simon finds that oil-based clay makes a good medium for transferring images to paper. It's versatile enough to accept a range of surface treatments, pliant yet sturdy enough to hold many shapes, and suitable for inking with printer's ink. In this project Lenore applies texture to a piece of clay, uses a paper pattern to shape it, inks it, and prints it. In the final work, one of a series entitled *Symbols of My People*, she also uses a roller to add a broad sweep of color in the background.

Step 1 The artist creates a relief pattern on a slab of oil-based clay by rolling a textured drinking glass over it. She presses firmly to ensure that the pattern is evenly transferred to the clay.

Step 2 After cutting out a pattern from scrap paper, Lenore shapes the clay by cutting around the pattern and removes the excess clay.

Step 3 Then the artist coats the shaped clay with a layer of water-based printer's ink applied with a roller.

Step 4 The inked shape is then laid on the artwork and pressed firmly in place so that the image is evenly transferred to the paper.

Step 5 One of a series of pieces called *Symbols of My People,* this work includes broad, variegated swirls of color in the background. Lenore created them using a roller.

Step 6 Another example of using a roller to apply printer's ink is *A Hose Is a Hose Is a Hose.* Lenore completed this 20′×30′ monoprint in 1983, and it is now in a private collection.

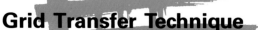

Nita Leland

Watercolor Artist
Dayton, Ohio

"It's customary for artists to work out their designs in thumbnail sketches—small roughs showing the division of space and placement of major shapes," relates watercolorist and art teacher Nita Leland. "Enlarging the sketch to the size required for the art may result in distortion if the two have different proportions."

To eliminate that possibility and ensure an easy transition from sketch to final artwork every time, Nita uses the tested technique of enlarging a sketch based on a grid. Here's how she does it: After determining the size of her final work, she selects the corresponding size for her sketch from a template she has prepared with several proportional windows and traces the appropriate window. Then she does her preliminary sketches based on these dimensions. After she chooses the sketch she wants to paint, she draws a grid pattern on the sketch and then transfers the drawing grid by grid to her final illustration board or watercolor paper.

"When I plan to use an unusual format not represented on the template, for example, one that is long and narrow," she explains, "I place the rough sketch in one corner of the larger piece of paper and measure a diagonal through the corners of the sketch to the top or side edge of the paper. The correct proportions for the enlarged drawing may be located at any point on this diagonal."

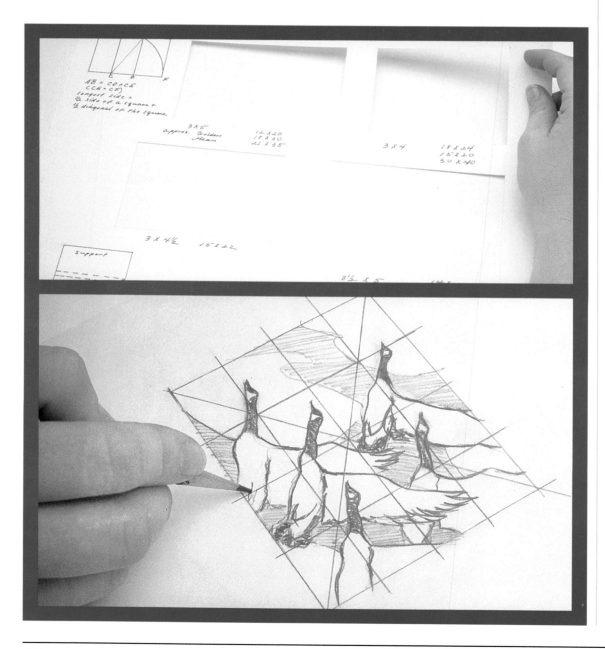

Step 1 Nita cuts windows in a template of heavy paper and labels them with paper sizes proportional to each space. The one on the upper left shows the sizes that correspond to the ideal proportions of the golden mean. The other three windows are standard sizes of watercolor papers that Nita uses most frequently in her work. After deciding the size of her painting, she traces the related window in the template several times so she can do a few sketches.

Step 2 After roughing out several sketches within the proportional rectangles, she selects the one she likes best for her final work. She draws a grid pattern on the sketch.

Step 3 Now she's ready to transfer the sketch to the final illustration board or paper. With a light pencil line, she draws a proportional grid pattern on her board or paper and copies the rough sketch, carefully transferring one grid at a time.

However, sometimes she varies this technique. "If I am using transparent watercolor rather than an opaque medium, I don't draw the grid on the paper or board. If the grid isn't completely erased or if the surface of the paper is altered by era-sure, some marks might show through the transparent washes. Instead I do the grid and drawing on tracing paper or newsprint the size of my illustration board. Then I place graphite transfer paper between the tracing paper drawing and the watercolor paper or board and outline the drawing (but not the grid) using just enough pressure to transfer the drawing to the final surface. It's like making a carbon copy of the drawing."

Step 4 When the design has been completely transferred to the final paper or illustration board, Nita finishes the work. This engaging watercolor is entitled *Rushing Wings*.

Robert Hudnall

Graphic Designer
Lubbock, Texas

Maybe it's because Robert Hudnall lives in an area that has a small graphics market and lacks most support systems that big-city designers take for granted that Robert has learned to be inventive and resourceful during his nearly 20-year career as a graphic designer in Lubbock, Texas. Putting his photographic skills to use in this secret, Robert has devised a method of preparing a complicated piece of airbrush artwork in perspective—quickly, accurately, and without grids or guesswork. The only special piece of equipment used is a 4"×5" camera fitted with a Polaroid back, but any good 35mm or medium-format camera could be substituted. After enlarging the Polaroid image on a stat camera, you photocopy it on a sheet of special removable material—Robert uses Crack'n Peel Plus (which acts like a decal or bumper sticker), though there are a number of brands of heat-proof, adhesive, peel-and-apply material. This becomes your frisket. In no time your artwork in perspective is ready to be sent to the client.

Step 1 Prepare your original line art at a comfortable, workable size. This will be determined primarily by the limits of your equipment.

Step 2 Position and secure the art to a stable surface, making careful note of the direction of the perspective. Although Robert photographed the art flat for this project, it could have been wrapped around a cylinder or bent around a corner for added dimensional effects. Using a light source that produces bright, even illumination is essential. Robert used a common fluorescent-and-tungsten drafting lamp. He determined the exposure of 4 seconds at f32 with a light meter and an 18% gray card, and he used a 4"×5" press camera with a Polaroid back, though any good 35mm or medium-format camera could be used. Says Robert, "The main advantage of using the 4"×5" was the Polaroid PN film, which produces a high-quality print and negative in seconds without a darkroom."

"The Polaroid print was sharp and contrasty, so there was no need to make an enlargement from the negative," states Robert. "If an enlargement had been needed I would have printed it on a grade 5 paper and retouched any flaws." Next Robert had a stat made of the print at 400%. Then he photographed the stat on a sheet of Crack'n Peel Plus.

Robert warns: "Ordinary photocopiers use heat and pressure to bond the toner to the paper. For this procedure the heat must be lowered to prevent melting the adhesive. Just ask the person running the photocopier to turn down the thermostat." Robert learned this the hard way: "One time the adhesive oozed all over the inside of the photocopier machine." But he adds, "Though this is a slightly risky stunt, it can be a real time-saver."

Step 3 Adhere the Crack'n Peel to the board and proceed as you would with any frisket.

Step 4 Advises Robert, "It's best not to leave Crack'n Peel on the board for more than a day or two. The older it gets the harder it sticks."

The Crack'n Peel is stable enough to be picked up and replaced repeatedly, and the tone repels water-based paint so you don't lose your guidelines if you happen to overspray.

Step 5 The intricate artwork is finished with perfect perspective but without the guesswork.

Carla Scornavacco

Graphic Designer
The Townsend Agency, Ltd.
Rosemont, Illinois

"You can photocopy a design or lettering right on your frisket paper while it is still on the backing," says graphic designer Carla Scornavacco. "Even though you may be limited by size, depending on your photocopier you can always copy sections at a time."

Carla explains how she invented this technique: "I tried this for the first time when I was airbrushing a 'Just Married' sign for my wedding. It saved a lot of time because I didn't have to hand letter first. It also gave me a more accurate image to cut from than one produced by a carbon transfer. When you're pressed for time, whether it be for a comp or final art, this technique is a great time-saver."

In this example Carla uses the instant frisket method twice to create a drop-shadow effect with lettering.

Step 1 Photocopy your image onto a sheet of frisket paper. Before handfeeding it into the photocopier, cover one edge with masking tape so the machine will be able to grip it.

Step 2 Remove the backing on the frisket paper, and position the image on your layout. Lightly cut along the edges of the lettering and remove the frisket to expose the letters.

Step 3 Airbrush the image.

Step 4 To add a drop shadow, trace the outline of the image, and photocopy it on to frisket paper using the same procedure as in Step 1.

Step 5 Position the outlined image as in Step 2, making sure to cut and remove the frisket only from the drop shadow areas.

Step 6 Airbrush the drop shadow in a softer shade of the color you used in Step 3, and finish the background using any airbrush technique you wish. Carla laid down a coat of flat color and then stippled over it with another color. (See Secret 34, Fantastik Airbrush Backgrounds, pages 62–65 for an innovative airbrush background technique.)

Scott Conrad

Artist and Photographer
Scott Conrad Art Services
Stone Mountain, Georgia

"Creating photograms for graphic designs is often overlooked by most artists, even though it's quick, fun, and easy," observes freelance artist and photographer Scott Conrad. "A photogram is a silhouette image of an object that is produced by placing it on a sheet of photographic paper and exposing it to light. Although a photographic process, no camera or enlarger is needed. All the materials you need are inexpensive and easily obtained from most camera stores: two trays, developer, fixer, a pack of high-contrast 8″×10″ photographic paper, and a darkroom safelight. You'll also need a room that can be used as a darkroom—a bathroom works well."

Any item that is opaque and lays flat can be used to create a photogram. Scott's favorite subjects are leaves, which he incorporated here into a logo for a landscaping company, but many applications are possible for border designs or as spot illustrations. The simple technique requires only a few minutes. Lay the object on a piece of photographic paper, expose it for a few seconds, and develop the image. "This produces a negative image, which may be desirable in some cases," Scott notes. "However, converting it to a positive takes only one more step."

Step 1 Before you begin, make sure your darkroom is as light-proof as possible. With the room lights out and the safelight on, place your image on a sheet of photographic paper—Scott finds high-contrast 8″×10″ paper meets most of his needs—and cover it with a sheet of clean glass to hold it flat. Turn on the overhead light bulb for a few seconds to expose the paper. It may be necessary to experiment a few times before you get an exposure you like.

Step 2 Develop the photogram as you would any photographic image. At this stage your image is a negative. You may choose to stop here.

Step 3 To produce a positive image, take the negative and a new sheet of photographic paper and place the emulsion sides facing each other, with the new sheet on the bottom—the light needs to pass through the original onto the new sheet of paper. Cover the two sheets with the glass, and make a longer exposure than in Step 1. The light needs more time to pass through the original opaque print. Develop as before and retouch as needed when dry. Note that while your image is now positive it is *flopped*.

Step 4 Photograms add decorative elements to graphic designs, as in this particularly apt logo for a nature-oriented company.

Mark Allison

Designer and Illustrator
Bishop, California

Like many freelancers, designer and illustrator Mark Allison is often pressed for time and money. The client wants to pay as little as possible for a job done yesterday. One way Mark has found to cut both corners is to eliminate halftones in his work. He converts drawings to line art by photocopying them. "This method is particularly suitable for small-run printing jobs that use a paper plate or even lower-cost printing using a photocopier," reports Mark. "Flyers and newspaper display ads are best suited to this method." An additional advantage is that the photocopier often alters the image in the process, introducing a slightly new and different texture or mood.

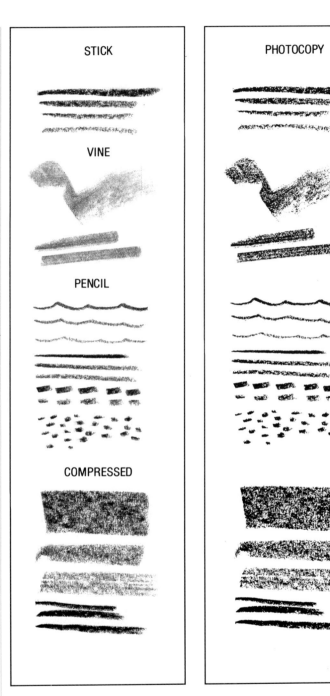

STICK

VINE

PENCIL

COMPRESSED

PHOTOCOPY

Copyright-free art, such as this drawing, makes a viable candidate for this technique, especially if you are on a tight budget and cannot afford halftones.

This charcoal drawing on bond paper was done for an ad that was needed in a hurry. Mark blended the charcoal with a paper stump in the background areas. The illustrator likes the effect created in the photocopy: "It looks like a litho stone drawing done with a grease crayon."

Vine charcoal, charcoal sticks and pencils offer unique, individual effects through this technique. Play with whatever kind of charcoal you have. Vary the pressure and stroke width. Vary even the darkness or lightness of the photocopy.

Tom O'Leary

Manager of Graphic Services
Blue Cross of Western
Pennsylvania
Pittsburgh, Pennsylvania

"We do a lot of 35mm slide work, and many a time we are looking for odd backgrounds to give dull presentations a lift," explains Tom O'Leary, manager of graphic services for Blue Cross's Pittsburgh office. "So I came up with the off-the-wall idea of using cigarette filter tips as an art tool." And it worked. Though Tom is proud to note that he quit smoking over a year ago, he now raids his wife's ashtray whenever he needs a new supply of filters. He has experimented with new and used filters and finds both work equally well. His only caution is not to pick up stray butts!

After you remove the filter paper with an X-Acto knife, you simply dip or soak the spongy filter in ink or paint—O'Leary used watercolors for this sample—and you're ready to work. "I don't consider a filter a serious tool, but more a fun thing," states Tom, who enjoys the freedom of working spontaneously. "By having a bowl or jar full of filters, you can use as many colors as you want without having to clean brushes, since each is disposable after one use."

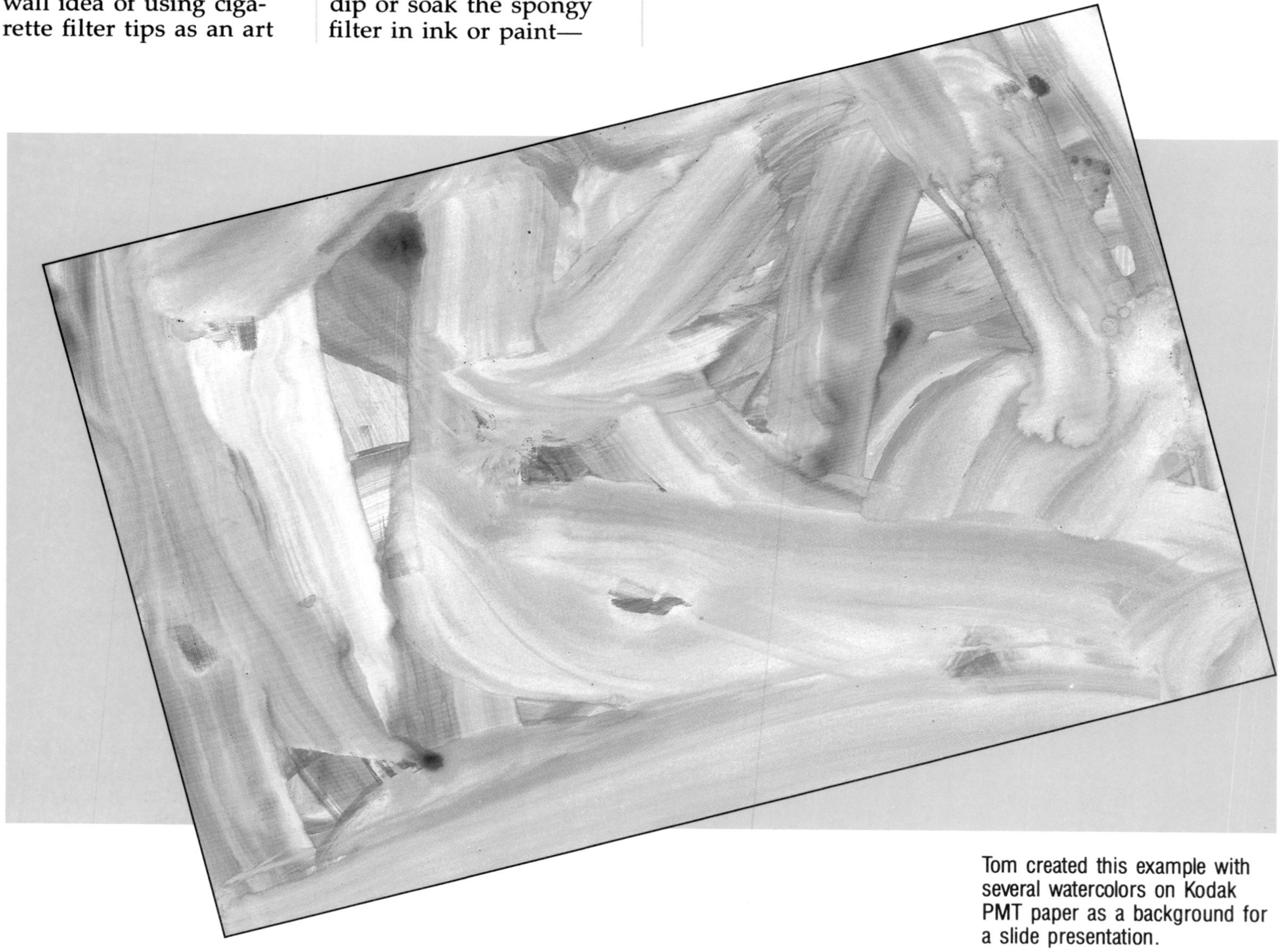

Tom created this example with several watercolors on Kodak PMT paper as a background for a slide presentation.

Richard E. McVicker

Patent Illustrator
Indianapolis, Indiana

As a patent draftsman, illustrator Richard McVicker is often called upon to draw consistent wavy lines in exact, detailed drawings. The ingenious technique he has perfected for doing that might merit a patent itself.

Richard takes the metal tear strip off a box of aluminum foil or wax paper and uses the serrated edge as a template. To apply ink for printing, he holds the pen as far away from the edge as possible and exerts a minimum of pressure against the strip. Different sizes of strips, which vary from product to product, yield diverse results. You may want to experiment with several strips to create your own exciting variations of this technique.

Step 1 Take the metal tear strip off a box of aluminum foil or wax paper. Note that different size serrated edges produce different results.

Step 2 It's easy to use the tear strip as a template for simple effects.

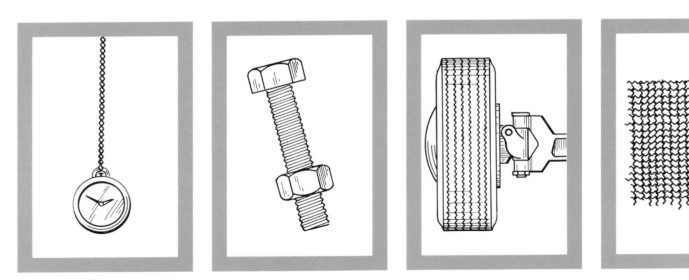

This chain was made in 15 seconds by simply reversing the serrated edge.

The technique is particularly time-saving for such minute and exacting work as bolt treads.

You can draw tire treads by taping the strip to a triangle and advancing it at regular intervals across the tire surface.

It's easy to create a controlled pattern, as shown here, by using an edge taped to a triangle. Actual drawing time for this pattern was three minutes.

55 Rubylith's Multiple Uses

Maria Carmer Webb

Art Director
Goodrich Marketing &
Advertising, Inc.
Coos Bay, Oregon

"My studio secret is very simple, but broad in application," reveals art director Maria Carmer Webb. "I use rubylith as a frisket. Just cut, spray or paint, and peel away. Then the acetate—the rubylith's backing sheet—can be spattered coarsely, sprayed finely, painted over, or resist-treated right up against solid masses, all with sharp edges and perfect registration. Edges never blow out, there's virtually no clean up, and the acetate is flexible. Besides obvious creative possibilities, a rubylith frisket is useful as a unique method of stencil preparation (for hand-done film positives) and amazingly practical for promotional sign work."

This technique has many applications, especially in advertising where Maria works. She recommends it for illustrations, promotions, point-of-purchase displays, one-of-a-kind projects, and also as a presentation, visualization, or color selection tool. "Its primary value to me as an art director is in color separations. Each color can have an airbrushed or painted appearance, and colors can overlap with no registration worries." And she adds, "If you give it your all, it often turns into art."

Step 1 Place a sheet of rubylith over your line drawing and tape them together at the top. Sometimes, you can skip this step and draw directly on the rubylith with a technical pen. This may be helpful if you want to flop all or part of the image, since you can write or draw on the back.

Step 2 Cut out all the areas that are to receive paint, ink, or spray paint. Even though rubylith is easy to cut, take your time and avoid unnecessary cut lines in the acetate. It's best to cut in the center of each line.

Step 3 Remove the film from the areas you wish to color and apply the spray. There is no limit to the colors you can use. With film positives, as shown here, and promotional signwork, only one area is involved, but when working creatively you may choose to open up a succession of layers. You can also experiment within the open areas with resists, such as glue, rubber cement, or those produced with a sponge.

Step 4 Remove the remaining rubylith, to expose the rest of the acetate, and your artwork is complete.

Maria produced all the sand and water positives in this print with her rubylith frisket technique. She needed at least ten different layers of rubylith to complete the complicated design. This work is now touring the Northwest in a marine art and science exhibit sponsored by the Coos Art Museum.

Anni Matsick

Illustrator
State College, Pennsylvania

Anni Matsick is quick to admit that even children in nursery school know how to spatter paint. How she applies the spattering technique—by making her own sheets of textured material—transforms it into a highly useful, versatile procedure that any designer can use to enhance an ink drawing. "This method of applying tone to your ink line art gives an unusual, personalized effect, rather than the standard dot patterns or other textures on commercially available transfer sheets," explains Anni, who specializes in illustrations for children's publications. "An added advantage is that I can prepare a number of sheets of texture at a time and keep them on file. Then they're ready

when I need them."

Spattering is particularly effective as a background panel, Anni finds. It can also be used as a drop shadow or can be applied to areas to suggest various textures. Simply take a sheet of spattered texture that has been prewaxed or sprayed with adhesive, mount it over your line art on a light table, cut out the desired area, and burnish it in position. Additional applications of the technique include applying a light spattering directly to finished art and using spattering as an overlay.

Anni's only note of caution is to be sure to test the texture before using it in an illustration. Copying it on a photocopier or photostat machine will show whether smaller dot patterns can be picked up by a camera.

Step 1 The basic materials needed to prepare spattered texture are a toothbrush, a stick, India ink in a saucer, and a sheet of 100-percent cotton tracing vellum (which is thin but won't ripple when wet). Begin by dipping the toothbrush bristles in the ink. Drag the edge of a stick along the bristles to spatter the ink. You can use any implement for this, so you may want to experiment with different tools to discover the range of effects you can create.

Step 2 Determine the right amount of ink and distance from the paper on a practice sheet; then switch to the vellum. To avoid puddling, it's best to stop and allow the ink to dry before applying another coat for a dense pattern. Let the sheet dry thoroughly before applying wax or repositionable spray adhesive to the back of the paper.

Now the texture is ready to use, or it can be stored. Note how much you can vary the effects with this technique from sparse to dense textures.

SPARSE

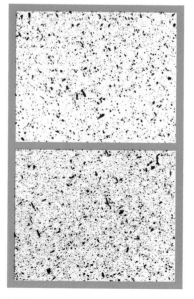

MEDIUM

DENSE

Step 3 This example shows three ways of using spattered texture: (from the left) as a background, as a drop shadow, and as texture in clothing.

Dear Mom, Please help Love Jennifer

'84 Iowa Freedom Bowl Tour

Travel with the Hawks to sunny Southern California!

The textured background adds depth to this drawing; it also silhouettes the figure, thus strengthening the foreground.

Used on the cover of a travel brochure, this illustration is a particularly appropriate use of the technique. The light covering of dots, added loosely after the drawing was completed, vividly conveys the dirt kicked up on a football field.

Step 1 Spattered texture can also be applied to an overlay and then reversed out during printing. Here the artist is planning to cover this line drawing (left and below) for a calendar with an overlay of white paint to indicate snow in the printed piece.

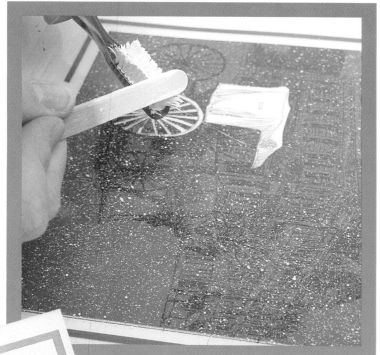

Step 2 The artist spatters white paint on a sheet of amber rubylith that has been registered over the black line art.

Step 3 The printer shoots the overlay for tone and combines it with the line shot.

Peter Bagnolo

Chairman (Coordinator)
Advertising Design and
Illustration Program
College of DuPage
Glen Ellyn, Illinois

If you need to sharpen your drawing skills, professor and former advertising executive Peter D. Bagnolo has a technique that's guaranteed to improve your work. "In the college where I teach we use the hyperaccurate drawing method called 'angular construction' in beginning illustration classes, and student drawing skills have increased from a 20% accuracy level to where 75% of the students now draw accurately with this method."

Based on the traditional principle of mathematical proportions, the illustrator superimposes a fairly elaborate grid system—called a "spline" grid after the computer pixel-averaging process from which it was derived—over a photograph and draws each section in great detail. "Once two points have been established on a drawing, they can be used to find other points from which you can build a well-organized, correctly constructed figure," explains Peter. "The essence of this technique is that the angle between a grid line and any line created by two points remains constant regardless of the difference in size of the two grids. Having a constant angle allows a proportional transfer, ensuring accuracy. This is not unlike the method originated by the ancient Greeks for drafting a curve."

Unlike the more informal enlarging method described by Nita Leland in Secret 48, this technique, which can be used for either enlarging or reducing, is specifically designed to yield highly realistic results.

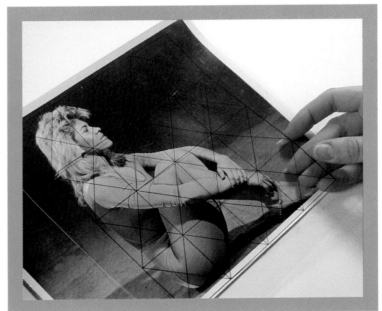

Step 1 Here is the photo from which Mary Lynne Sullivan, a student of Peter's at the College of DuPage, made the final illustration.

Step 2 This shows the photograph covered with an acetate grid; acetate, rather than tissue, was used so you can clearly see detailing in the photo. The sidebar on page 116 shows how to construct the basic grid. Note that you need two grids at this stage: one on acetate to cover the photo and one on tissue for your drawing.

Step 3 You're ready to start the drawing. Begin by locating the point in the photograph where the top of the head touches the top line of the acetate grid. Mark that point on your tissue grid. Go back to the photograph and locate that point again. Place your drawing pencil down with the tip over that point on the photo and angle it from that point down to the end of the hair over the model's forehead. Holding your pencil at that angle, move it over to your drawing grid and establish the point of the end of the hair on your drawing. Now draw a line connecting the two points. This gives you an accurate line for the top of the head. Now establish other points and lines in the same manner.

Move down both sides of the body, developing the entire outline as you go. In that way you can establish some sense of balance and consistency. Use both the intersections on the grid and reference points on the body to locate the points. The easiest points to find are those that indicate a change of line or plane direction, like joints. Remember that you only need to project two points at a time.

Constructing Your Grid

To put this secret to work for you, you will need to draw two grids: one on acetate the size of the subject in your photograph and another on tissue proportional to the acetate grid but the size of your drawing. The following step-by-step demonstration shows you the method for creating both grids.

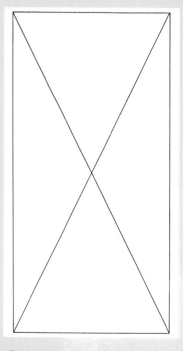

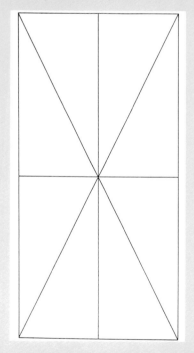

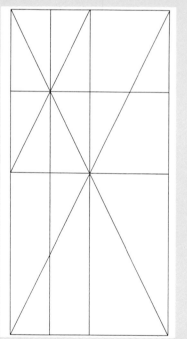

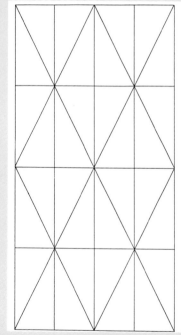

Step 1 Using a technical pen on acetate, begin making the grid for your illustration by drawing a rectangle the same size as the subject in your photograph. Draw a diagonal line from the top left-hand corner to the bottom right-hand corner and another one connecting the opposite corners.

Step 2 Where the lines cross in the center, draw a horizontal line and a vertical line. This creates four rectangles that evenly divide the larger rectangle.

Step 3 Now beginning with the upper left section of the rectangle, draw a diagonal from the upper right-hand corner to the lower left-hand corner. Where that line crosses the first diagonal, draw vertical and horizontal lines, creating four more rectangles.

Step 4 Now continue to fill in each of the three remaining rectangles with diagonals, horizontals, and verticals. Your grid is now evenly divided into four vertical and four horizontal sections.

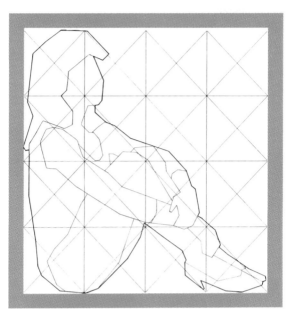

Step 4 Once the entire outline of the figure is completed, you're ready to begin adding details. As you did before, start with the head and work down the body.

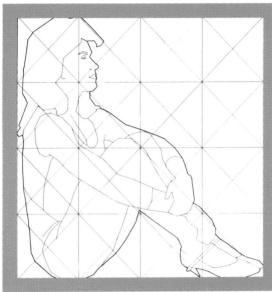

Step 5 In constructing smaller details, like the facial features shown here, it helps to refer to as many points on the grid as possible. Continue working down the figure. It gets easier to establish points and connect them the more practice you have.

Step 6 Now add more exact details for greater refinement. Introduce as many details as you want at this stage; they will help you refine the final drawing.

Once your drawing is completed, you're ready to transfer the drawing from the tissue to your final illustration board and add tone and shading to finish the piece. Peter recommends hot-press illustration board for a more photographic-looking drawing.

Transferring Your Drawing

Turn your tissue drawing over and, on the back, go over the flopped image with a 4B pencil so you have a clean, thick black line. Turn your drawing back to the right side and tape it to your final illustration board at all four corners. Softly retrace the image with a sharp 2H pencil, being careful not to press too hard, which would ruin the board. Check the transferred image by untaping the bottom two corners and raising the tissue. You can repeat this step as many times as needed; just make sure not to let the tissue slip out of alignment with your illustration board. Clean up the image with a kneaded eraser and, if necessary, redraw with a sharp 2H pencil. Now you're ready to add tone and shadow.

Step 7 This is Mary Lynne Sullivan's expert drawing.

58 Computer Art Shortcut

Donald Feight

Technical Illustrator and
Commercial and Graphic Artist
Lockheed Corporation
Manchaca, Texas

Just as computers are
radically changing all
kinds of data processing,
they are also having a
decisive effect on design.
Now images can be sent
around the world in sec-
onds or manipulated and
altered with the touch of
a few specially designed
keys (see Secret 26, for
example). No doubt
about it, computers have
become the designer's
newest, most sophisti-
cated graphic arts tool.

This technique of trans-
ferring an illustration
from a magazine or book
to a computer for adapta-
tion or refinement can
help you if your office
doesn't yet have a scan-
ner. Donald Feight, who
is a technical illustrator at
Lockheed, recommends it
"for anything you use
your computer for—art
for proposals or presentations, flyers, or in-house
documents."

Step 1 Copy your art onto a
transparent medium specially
made for use in a photocopier.
If you don't have any handy and
you're in a rush, use a sheet of
acetate by covering one edge
with masking tape, as described
in Secret 50, Faster-Yet Design
Transfer.

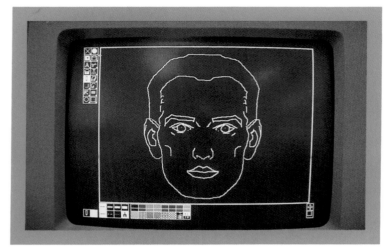

Step 2 By taping the acetate to
your computer screen you can
easily trace the image.

Step 3 The traced artwork may
be modified or altered to suit
any need.

Step 4 Here is the final artwork, which has been consider-
ably changed and refined.

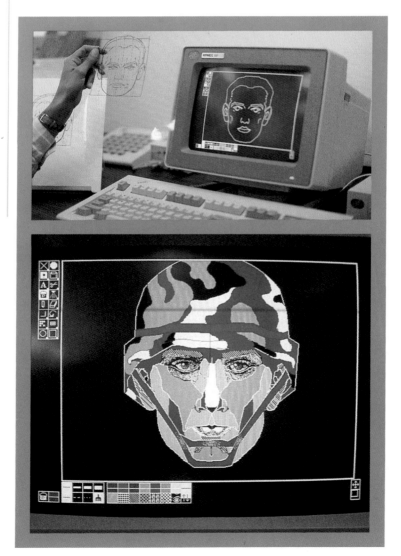

Joe Lertola

Illustrator
Time
New York, New York

You know those clever charts in *Time?* When they were first introduced at least ten years ago by illustrator Nigel Holmes, they transformed the task of presenting statistics—a notoriously dull subject—into a skillful art and revolutionized chart making in the process. Illustrator Joe Lertola is currently carrying on that tradition.

One of the newest tools of his trade is a Macintosh computer. Driven by a fascination with computers as well as by a demanding job, Joe began investigating different kinds of software. One program that he found particularly suited to his kind of technical illustration work is Adobe Illustrator 88—a program that gives precise control over the drawings and produces high-resolution images on a laser printer. "With Illustrator I can produce many of the illustrations I used to do by hand in *minutes,* cutting the time needed to create finished art. One thing I often want to do in an illustration is add depth to a shape by creating a three-dimensional shadow. Instead of spending hours doing it, this drawing took me only 25 minutes on the computer. Although this procedure may seem tedious to a beginner, when you are familiar with the program, it goes very fast."

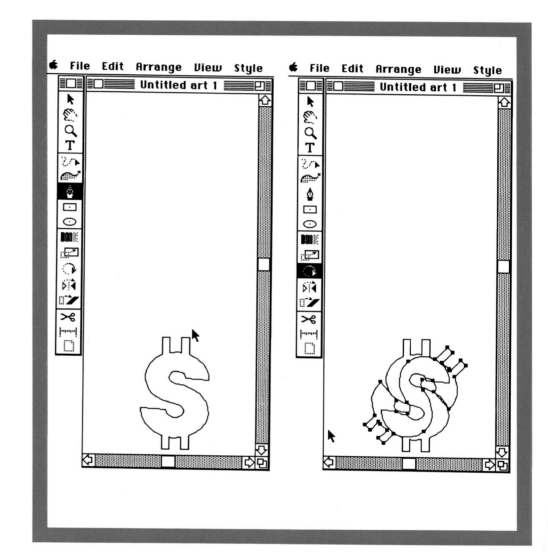

Step 1 Joe first drew the outline of a dollar sign with the drawing tool. Note that the Adobe's different functions are keyed to special symbols shown to the left of the artwork. Seventh down from the top, the drawing tool is aptly denoted with the nib of a pen.

Step 2 Joe decides it will be easier to work on the drawing at an angle. In order to turn the dollar sign, he has to "select" it by positioning the pointing tool (first tool from the top) on the dollar sign and clicking the mouse button. This creates the tiny black "diamonds" or "handles," which allow him to use the rotation tool (sixth from the bottom) to tilt the drawing.

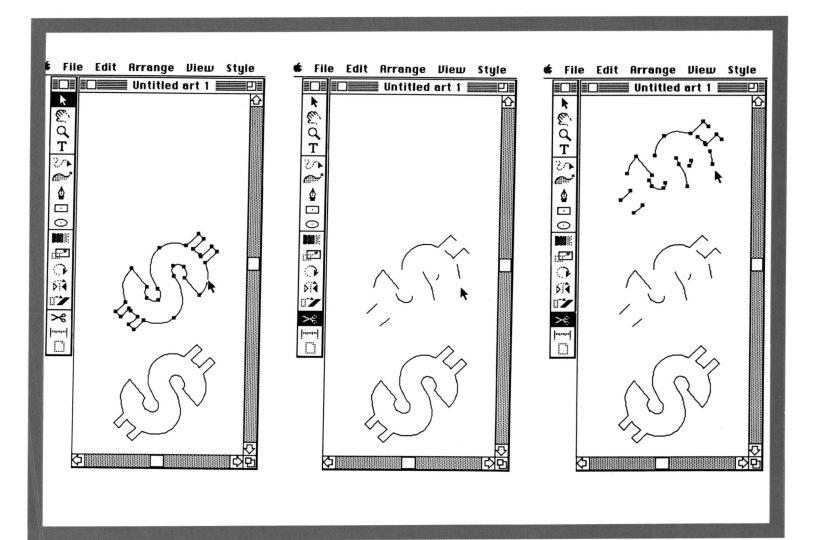

Step 3 To have enough space to create the dimensional effect behind the dollar sign, the illustrator needs to reposition the image. He clicks on the object with the pointing tool and, while simultaneously holding down the mouse button, the keyboard shift key, and the option key, he "drags" the image up. The shift key moves the outline up vertically while the option key makes a copy of it above the original.

Step 4 Using the scissors tool (third from the bottom), Joe cuts away all the parts of the object that are facing down.

Step 5 Joe wants to duplicate the remaining lines, so after selecting them with the pointing tool, he again holds down the shift and option keys and moves the image up. "Leave plenty of space between the two images," he cautions, "so they won't interfere with each other."

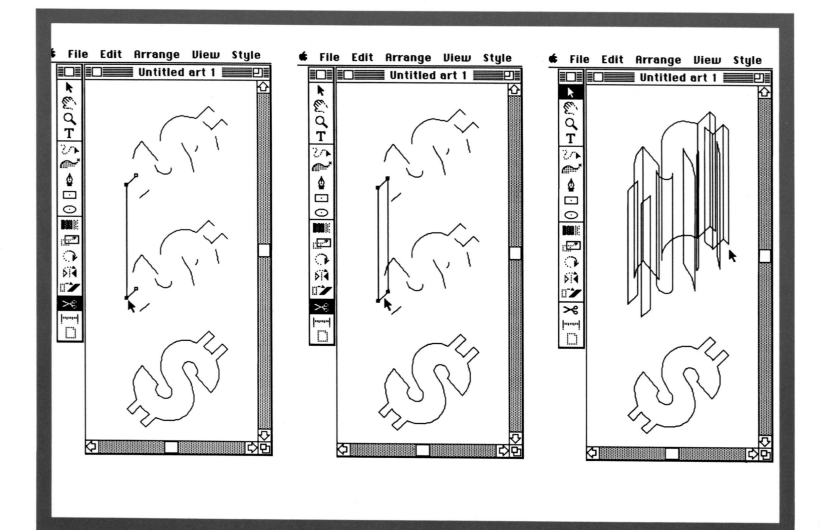

Step 6 Using the pointing tool, the illustrator selects the end handles of two corresponding lines and joins them by using the join function under the Arrange menu. (This menu shows up on the screen when the pointer is placed on the word *Arrange* at the top and the mouse button is held down.)

Step 7 Joe selects the other two handles and joins them, thus forming a closed shape.

Step 8 The illustrator continues this process until all the lines are joined.

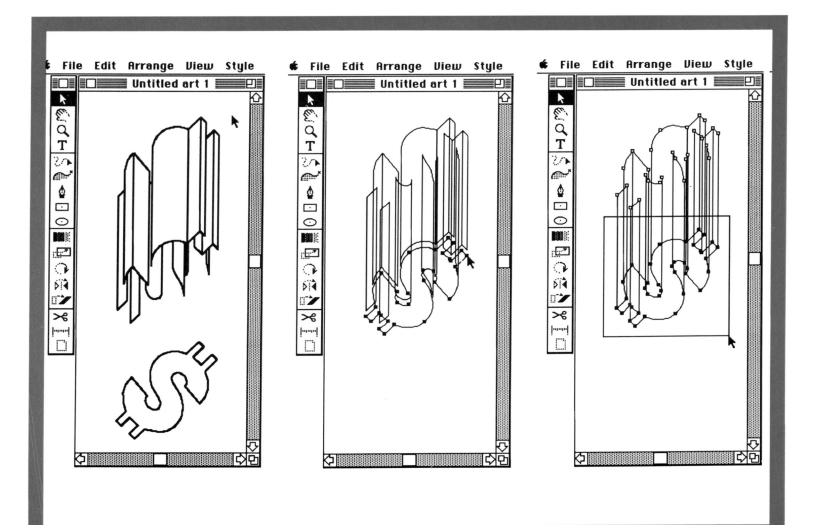

Step 9 Next Joe previews the image, by selecting Preview from the View menu above, to make sure all the shapes are in the right order, one on top of another. "If they are not," Joe notes, "rearrange them by selecting one or more and moving them to the top or bottom as needed."

Step 10 Now the illustrator is ready to merge the two remaining images. He selects the dollar sign with the pointing tool, and drags it up while holding down the shift key to the corresponding point on the shadow. When it is close enough, the computer will automatically snap it into place. Then Joe uses two commands from the Edit menu, above—(1) cut and paste and (2) front—so the dollar sign will be in front of the shadow.

Step 11 To adjust the depth of the shadow, the illustrator begins by using the pointer to create a selection rectangle around the points on the lower half of the dollar sign.

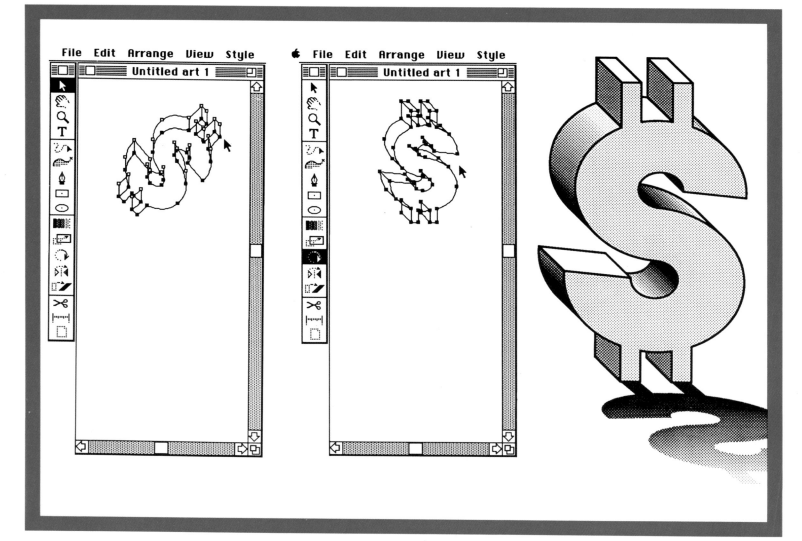

Step 12 Joe then selects the face of the dollar sign and drags it vertically until the shadow is the right depth. Only the shift key is used for this.

Step 13 Joe uses the rotation tool to move the dollar sign back to an upright position. Note that the entire dollar sign is selected in order to do this.

Step 14 To complete the illustration, Joe uses several other options on the Illustrator program to create a gradated ground shadow and to add tone to the sign to enhance the three-dimensional effect.

Now that you've discovered a range of more complex ways to illustrate your designs using the thirty-three secrets in this section, here are six additional working tips that can save you time and effort.

Tips for Different Media

Lisa Blackshear
Illustrator and Painter
New York, New York

Lisa Blackshear, New York City illustrator and painter, has six tips for working with different media:
• If you make a mistake in airbrush, you can scrape off the surface of the paper with a very sharp X-Acto knife. It helps if you use a good-quality paper like Strathmore 500 with a high rag content.
• To get a spatter effect using an airbrush, turn the pressure on the compressor down to 5 pounds per square inch.
• To control toothbrush spattering, you can use frisket paper for a mask and spatter on to white scratchboard or Caslon airbrush paper. Then scratch off undesired portions of the spatter with an X-Acto knife.
• To highlight areas in watercolor painting, you can scrub off color with a wet toothbrush, varying your technique depending on the effect you want to create.
• If you want to slow down the drying time of watercolor, add a little glycerin to your paint. To make watercolors blend better, add some Photo-flo to your colors.
• If you want to exploit the deckled edge of watercolor paper, but you don't want your painting to wrinkle or buckle, you can flatten your work using this method. Place the finished painting face down on a piece of glass that is slightly bigger than the painting. Moisten the back of the painting with a wet sponge and then place the moist side down on a piece of unfinished plywood or particle board, placing the glass over the face of the illustration. Put weights, such as books, on the glass, and leave it for one to three days. The moisture will evaporate through the board, and your painting will be as flat as if you had stretched it.

Photo Retouching Tip

Robert Hudnall
Graphic Designer and Illustrator
Lubbock, Texas

When retouching photographs with an airbrush or illustrating on a smooth surface, it is sometimes necessary to use a fixative or retouch lacquer in order to get pencil or pastel to adhere to the surface. The problem is that the fixative or lacquer often causes gouache to change color or become transparent. Robert Hudnall's solution is to seal the surface with a light spray of gum arabic.

First Aid for Painted Cats

Patie Kay
Graphic Artist
Pico Rivera, California

Graphic artist Patie Kay has come up with an ingenious six-step procedure for removing paint from a cat. "This remedy was hastily improvised when my six-month-old kitten, Cyrano, sat none too artistically on my palette of oil paints," explains Patie. "Cyrano is not a fast learner, so we went through this procedure on two occasions. However, once he learns, he does remember. Eight years later he still stands on his hind legs as he scouts for a prospective landing area on any surface in my studio."

The following directions are for oil-based paints. For acrylic or any water-soluble paint, omit step 3. (1) Grab the cat *fast*. If the cat begins to lick the paint, it could do internal damage, or if she or he runs amuck, that could ruin your studio. (2) Place the cat's clean end under your arm, clamping the cat firmly to your side. Hold the back paws to keep the cat from scratching. (3) Dampen paper towels or a clean rag with paint thinner and stroke down the fur. Do not rub the fur; that works the paint into the fur and on to the skin. Remove as much paint as possible. (4) Move to the sink and hold the area under warm running water. Wash the area thoroughly with a gentle soap, such as Ivory. Rinse well. (5) Cover the wet area with clean towels and dry the cat as much as possible. (6) Use the warm setting on a blow dryer or hair dryer to finish drying and fluffing the fur.

Blending Pastel with Oil

Melody Joy Pickels
Instructor
Elmwood Park, New Jersey

Instructor Melody Joy Pickels enjoys working with Cray-Pas and pastels, but when she first began working with them, she was upset with breaks in the color she was laying down. Here's how she solved the problem: "Knowing that Cray-Pas has some oil in it, I experimented by adding a little bit more oil to it. Putting baby oil on a cotton swab and applying it lightly to the colored surface makes the Cray-Pas breakage disappear. It also helps blend different colors together." Melody has found this technique especially helpful for ocean scenes.

Safe and Simple Fixative

S. L. Baltrunas
Artist
Walla Walla, Washington

"I took a lesson from Degas and use very warm water as a fixative for all my working layers," says artist S. L. Baltrunas, describing his work in charcoal, Conté crayon, and pastel. He also works in oil, pen and ink, pencil, and watercolors. "I spray a fine mist over the work, allow it to dry, and apply a second coat of the medium. The beauty of this is that I can work the material while still wet to give an appearance of an oil painting if I choose. The colors do not darken as with conventional fixative, and only a very light coat of spray matte fixative is needed to fix the final coat. This has solved my problem of using a toxic aerosol in a closed space and gives my work a brighter, most pleasing appearance. For some reason it cured my migraine headaches too!"

Airbrushing Clouds

James Kilroy
Airbrush Artist and Designer
Pensacola, Florida

When airbrushing beach and sailboating scenes on T-shirts, artist and designer James Kilroy has come up with an ingenious way of creating clouds. He buys Pellon, sold as interfacing in fabric stores, and *tears* it into a rough cloud shape. "I lay the torn piece on the T-shirt and airbrush lightly around it, creating a natural-looking cloud. The rough edge and fibers make an extremely soft edge." Jim has used this technique with acrylic paints and fabric dyes and believes it will work equally well with watercolors.

Mark Allison
Route 1, Box K4, #37
Bishop, CA 93514

Mark Allison is a busy, successful designer and illustrator in Bishop, California, with eighteen years of experience in the field. Among the seventeen services listed on his business card are photography, packaging, technical/medical illustration, cartoon illustration, and 3-D models.

Robert Andraschko
RR #3, Box 99K
Winona, MN 55987

Robert Andraschko is currently a graphic arts instructor at Western Wisconsin Technical College in LaCrosse, Wisconsin. He used to work in the newspaper business as a production manager and assistant advertising manager.

John M. Angelini, AWS
12603 Pecan Tree Drive
Hudson, FL 34669

After a highly successful career in New Jersey as an art director and consultant for a major packaging company, John Angelini retired to Florida, where he continues to paint watercolors. A member of the American Watercolor Society since 1967, John has had numerous exhibitions throughout the northeast, and his work has won over 135 awards. He is the author of *The North Light Art Competition Handbook*.

Peter D. Bagnolo
College of DuPage
22nd Street and Lambert Road
Glen Ellyn, IL 60137

Peter D. Bagnolo has been chairman (coordinator) of the Advertising Design and Illustration program at the College of DuPage in Illinois since 1976. After seven years as vice president at a medium-sized Chicago advertising agency, Peter opened his own firm in 1973, finally retiring as chairman of the board in 1984. He earned an MA in graphic art and cultural anthropology from Goddard College in 1974.

S. L. Baltrunas
Box 520
Walla Walla, WA 99362

With a master's degree in fine arts, S. L. Baltrunas enjoys doing everything from oil and pastel portraits to commercial pen-and-ink sketches to wall murals in pastels.

Lisa Blackshear
530 Grand Street
New York, NY 10002

A graduate of the University of Minnesota in fine arts, Lisa Blackshear was the art director of a small weekly newspaper in Minneapolis before coming to New York as a freelance artist. Among her clients are the *Nation*, the *New York Press*, and the *New York Times*. Her work is shown in the Bridgewater Gallery in Manhattan.

Glenn Bookman
ARTWORKS Studio
175 Serrill Road
Elkins Park, PA 19117

Glenn Bookman is a versatile artist involved in all phases of creative graphic design including illustration, cartooning, point-of-purchase (P-O-P) displays, logos, signage, location photography, sculpting models, and art direction for television and film. He has several P-O-P displays in national and international distribution and has worked closely with manufacturers on new product development and marketing, notably in the gift and novelty industry.

Linda Bourke
1699 Cambridge Street
Cambridge, MA 02138

Linda Bourke is a freelance designer and illustrator. She has written and/or illustrated ten children's books, including *A Show of Hands* and *It's Your Move*. Linda received a BFA from Massachusetts College of Art of Boston, where she is presently on the faculty teaching illustration and drawing. She has an MFA in illustration from Syracuse University.

Howard F. Bradybaugh
Museum Graphics
1308 Rush Henrietta
Town Line Road
Rush, NY 14543

After graduating from an industrial arts high school with a major in drafting, Howard F. Bradybaugh spent over twenty-five years as a patent illustrator with the Xerox Corporation. He was supervisor of the Patent Illustration group at the time of his early retirement in 1987. Now he does consulting and patent drawing, specializing in graphics for museums. Howard perfected his secret while illustrating world airmail routes for the American Air Mail Society.

Deborah Brumfield
Brumfield Studios
Rural Route 1, Box 679-B
Route 123
Walpole, NH 03608

Deborah DeLisi Brumfield operates her own graphic design studio in Walpole, New Hampshire. She has been designing and producing logos, brochures, and related design projects over the past ten years. In 1976 Debbie graduated from the University of Bridgeport in Connecticut, where she earned an AA degree in advertising art. Her real education came from postgraduate experience as a television art director, ad agency designer, magazine production and ad designer, and a myriad of freelance assignments.

Steven Carroll
19 Simmons Circle
Doraville, GA 30340

Steven Carroll is a graduate of DeKalb College with over six years experience in print and television advertising. He is presently employed as the senior art director of Decker, Kelley & Brown advertising agency in Atlanta. Steven has done work for such clients as Coca Cola, Hitachi Power Tools, Yamaha Southeast, and Epson South.

Gisele C. Conn
75 Lakepines
Irvine, CA 92720

Gisele Conn works in the creative art department of the *Orange County Register* in Santa Ana, California. In 1988 she won first place for best special-section cover illustration in the Newspaper Advertising Co-op Network competition. Gisele earned a degree in advertising in Puerto Rico and has continued her study of fine art and graphic design in Puerto Rico and Chicago.

Jim Connelly
Airow Studio
4753 Byron Center
Wyoming, MI 49509

With over fifteen years of airbrush experience, Jim Connelly has operated Airow Graphics for the last three years. He supplies agencies, publishers, and industry with various airbrush services, including photo retouching, illustration, and lettering. "I enjoy the challenge of satisfying each client by meeting his

or her particular needs with great work."

Scott Conrad
Scott Conrad Art Services
4822 Rockbridge Road
Stone Mountain, GA 30083

Scott Conrad is a graduate of the Lane School of Art in Decatur, Georgia. He spent several years as an artist for a silk-screen printing company. Now he does freelance art and photography, in addition to serving as a part-time instructor at the Lane School of Art.

Stan H. Covington, Jr.
1305 Canterbury Lane
Colonial Heights, VA 23834

A veteran of World War II, Stan H. Covington, Jr. graduated from Richmond Professional Institute with a degree in commercial art. He worked for the Department of the Army for thirty-four years as an illustrator, designer, and visual information specialist. Now retired, he is writing and illustrating a history of his church.

Becky L. Craig
8825 Roswell Road, Suite 477
Atlanta, GA 30350

Becky L. Craig graduated from the Art Institute of Atlanta in 1975 and has worked for a number of publishers and advertising agencies as an artist and designer. Currently she is the art director of Shore Communications, Inc. Her cover designs and illustrations for Shore have won several awards from the American Society of Business Press Editors.

Doreen Curtin
P.O. Box 5453
Clinton, NJ 08809

Educated as both an artist and biologist, Doreen Curtin has dedicated her art skills to creating public awareness of the need for wildlife and environmental conservation. She does design and illustration for such organizations as the National Audubon Society, the New Jersey Endangered and Nongame Species Program, the Smithsonian Institution, and many zoological institutes. Currently she is devoting time to the problems of acid rain.

Tony DiLaurenzio
AD Art & Design
152 Ruland Road
Selden, NY 11784

After graduating from New York City Community College, Tony DiLaurenzio worked in studios and ad agencies and was the art director of two major toy corporations. He started his own studio in New York in 1969, but migrated to Long Island in 1980. Tony concentrates on design through finished art of sales promotion and packaging projects.

Kathy Dodd
9023 Diplomacy Row
Dallas, TX 75247

Kathy Dodd is the in-house artist for Berlin Printing Co. in Dallas, Texas, and during her spare time enjoys all types of arts and crafts. She attended Stephen F. Austin State College in Nacogdoches, Texas, where she studied all levels of art education.

Pete Dreger
Chicago Tribune
435 North Michigan Avenue
Chicago, IL 60611

Pete Dreger is a graphic designer working in advertising design at the *Chicago Tribune*.

James M. Effler
A.I.R. Studio
203 East 7th Street
Cincinnati, OH 45202

James Effler is a 1978 graduate of the Art Academy of Cincinnati, where he majored in graphic design and illustration. He joined David Miller in partnership in 1982 when they established A.I.R. Studio, Inc., which specializes in airbrush illustration. Examples of their award-winning work are featured in their book, *Dynamic Airbrush*.

Donald Feight
12400 Twin Creek Road
Manchaca, TX 78652

For the past fifteen years, Donald Feight has worked at Lockheed in California and Texas as a technical illustrator and commercial and graphic artist. He has an AA degree from San Jose City College. Donald enjoys doing freelance art of all types, but his favorites are railroad and aviation art.

Martha Galuszka
324 Oakwood Avenue
West Hartford, CT 06110

Martha Galuszka works as a partner in a four-person, full-service agency. With a background in fine art and a degree in art education, Martha feels she's come full circle since she began teaching airbrush painting on the side two years ago.

Isabel C. Guerra
276 Varick Street
Jersey City, NJ 07302

A graduate of the arts program at Cooper Union in New York City, Isabel Guerra is a freelance graphic designer who works part-time for Bevington Design, Inc., in Long Island City, New York. Isabel enjoys drawing and printmaking in her spare time.

Carol Hettenbach
First Exposure Graphics
10146 Burrock Drive
Santee, CA 92071

Carol Hettenbach is a freelance designer and photographer. After earning a degree in graphics from the Leeward Community College campus of the University of Hawaii, she opened her own studio, First Exposure Graphics, in California, where she specializes in fine art landscape and wildlife photography.

W. J. Hildebrandt
The Cellar Scriptorium
25 Beaverbrook Road
West Simsbury, CT 06092

After thirty-one years as an electrical engineer in new product research and development for major corporations in Connecticut, and with thirty-five patents in the mechanical and electronic arts to his credit, Bill Hildebrandt turned full-time to his lifelong hobby. He runs a calligraphic design service, The Cellar Scriptorium, teaches calligraphy, and is the proprietor of a private press. He invented the Whopper-plate pen and in 1987 published a collection of calligraphic parodies entitled *Songs of the Scribe*.

Robert Hudnall
P.O. Box 5724
Lubbock, TX 79417

Robert Hudnall graduated from Texas Tech University in 1970 with a BFA in graphic design and a minor in photography. Because he lives in a part of Texas that lacks the kinds of support systems most designers take for granted, Robert has often found himself working simultaneously as designer, illustrator, photographer, retoucher, copy or jingle writer, and gofer.

Kerry S. Jenkins
3226 Marlborough Road
Charlotte, NC 28208

Kerry Jenkins received a BFA with a graphic design concentration from Western Carolina University in 1985 after earning an AA degree in commercial graphics from McDowell Technical College. He is head of the Graphics Department of the North Carolina office of Arthur Anderson & Co., an audit, accounting, tax, and information consulting firm. Since he joined the company upon graduation, he has won two firmwide awards for marketing excellence. Kerry enjoys doing humorous illustration when he's not at work.

Robin Kappy
17 Greenwich Avenue
New York, NY 10014

Robin Kappy graduated from the Parsons School of Design in 1978 with a BFA in illustration. Since then, she has done design, production, and illustrations for such clients as Arnold Saks, Bankers Trust, and Equitable Life Assurance. "I'm a painter at heart," says Robin.

Patie Kay
4932 South Passons Boulevard
Pico Rivera, CA 90660

Patie Kay has been a professional freelance artist since 1976 and a published author since 1985. She is planning to move to Kingman, Arizona, where she intends to continue her art and writing.

James Kilroy
7601 North 9th Avenue
Pensacola, FL 32514

James Kilroy became interested in airbrush through model building. He has a degree in business and works in contract engineering.

Peter Kuper
250 West 99th Street
New York, NY 10025

While Peter Kuper was studying illustration at Pratt Institute in Brooklyn, New York, he worked as an assistant illustrator in a comic artist's studio in New York City. Peter supports himself by doing illustrations for such clients as *Business Week*, CBS Records, the *New York Times*, and *Time*. In his spare time Peter is co-publisher of *World War 3*, an underground comics-style magazine. A collection of his work, *New York, New York*, was published in 1988 by Fantagraphic Books.

Nita Leland
1210 Brittany Hills Drive
Dayton, OH 45459

A graduate of Otterbein College, watercolorist Nita Leland is the author of *Exploring Color* (North Light Books). She teaches at Riverbend Art Center in Dayton and critiques for the North Light Art School home study course. Nita also judges art exhibitions, lectures on the study and history of color in painting, and teaches comprehensive color workshops and watercolor classes.

Joseph Lertola
14 Horatio Street
New York, NY 10014

In addition to being a freelance artist, Joe Lertola is an illustrator at *Time* who specializes in detailed and imaginative charts and diagrams. After studying graphic design at Pratt Institute in Brooklyn, he worked as a mechanical artist for a number of years, moving increasingly in the direction of illustration.

David Lewis
429 Elm Avenue
Terrace Park, OH 45174

Before joining the editorial side of book publishing, David Lewis began his career in England as a graphic designer.

Steve McCue
3725 North Flowing Wells Road
Tucson, AZ 85705

A graduate of the University of Arizona, Steve McCue has been teaching art at Flowing Wells High School in Tucson for the past twenty years. His school district has won more state and national awards than any other school district in Arizona. "I like to think that I've been part of this success," says Steve.

Lachlan McIntosh
The Write Design
376 North Firestone Boulevard
Akron, OH 44301

Lachlan McIntosh believes that layout and design should help sell the product, not just look aesthetically

pleasing. He's been involved in different aspects of graphics for twenty-five years. Because he has a parallel career as a copywriter, he is able to offer unique services, such as writing and designing direct mail packages, which is one of his specialties. In addition, he helped create and produce one of the first home-shopping TV shows in the nation.

Richard E. McVicker
Barnes & Thornburg
1313 Merchants Bank Building
Indianapolis, IN 46204

Since Richard E. McVicker earned a vocational degree in drafting at Muncie Trade School in Indiana, he has worked for a number of major corporations and law firms. Currently he is a patent draftsman for the law firm of Barnes & Thornburg. McVicker stands by his design idea: "I have used this technique for twenty-five years in preparing official U.S. patent drawings."

Anni Matsick
345 Oakley Drive
State College, PA 16803

Anni Delsandro Matsick is a freelance illustrator whose work in ink and watercolor has appeared in numerous publications for children. She has illustrated many other kinds of printed material, including menus and brochures. Anni is a graduate of Carnegie-Mellon University's Department of Painting.

Barbara Matunas
Advertising-Marketing Resources
1855 Trawood
El Paso, TX 79935

Barbara Matunas received a BFA from the University of Texas at El Paso, with a major in metalsmithing and a minor in printmaking. She has also pursued Asian studies in both the United States and Asia; her special interests include Chinese brush painting and watercolors. After working for a small ad agency in El Paso, Barbara opened a graphic design studio in 1986 with two partners. The business offers full design and advertising services with an emphasis on print design.

Rose Mayer
Chicago Tribune
435 North Michigan Avenue
Chicago, IL 60611

Rose Mayer is a graphic designer who works on promotional materials for the *Chicago Tribune*. She also designs greeting cards and is developing an upcoming line.

Mark Mealy
1448 Church Street, NW
Washington, D.C. 20005

Mark Mealy is a 1985 graduate of the Parsons School of Design in New York City, with a BFA in environmental design. He works for Greenwell Goetz Architects, a large Washington, D.C.-based architectural firm. Mark uses his airbrush skills primarily in architectural renderings but notes that airbrushing also helps him in design development.

David Miller
A. I. R. Studio
203 East 7th Street
Cincinnati, OH 45202

David Miller attended the Art Academy of Cincinnati and then studied airbrush rendering and photo retouching. He established a partnership with James M. Effler in 1982. A. I. R. Studio, Inc., specializes in airbrush illustration, which is featured in their book, *Dynamic Airbrush*.

Mary Ann Nichols
Nichols Graphic Design
80 Eighth Avenue, Suite 1216
New York, NY 10011

Mary Ann Nichols is an award-winning graphic designer with her own studio in Manhattan. A native New Yorker, she is a graduate of Cooper Union and a member of the Art Directors Club of New York, the American Institute of Graphic Arts, Graphic Artists Guild, and Women's Direct Response Group.

Sharon L. Noel
137 Royal Avenue
Strasburg, VA 22657

A dreamer who claims to have doodled incessantly since birth, Sharon L. Noel works as a graphic designer and artist at Shenandoah Valley Press, Inc. Sharon says, "Printers insist I lie awake at night creating designs that simply *cannot* be printed . . . and I do! But my mother always told me, 'There's no such word as can't.' And somehow printers always come through with something they hadn't thought possible." Sharon also owns a graphic design company, Lasting Impressions graphic design.

Tom O'Leary
Graphic Services Department
Blue Cross of Western
Pennsylvania
Fifth Avenue Place
Pittsburgh, PA 15222

A graduate of the University of Pittsburgh Fine Arts Department, Tom O'Leary is a manager in the Graphic Services Department of Blue Cross in Pittsburgh.

Melody Joy Pickels
276 Martha Avenue
Elmwood Park, NJ 07407

After graduating from the Masters Institute in Lockhaven, Pennsylvania, with an AA degree in commercial art, Melody Joy Pickels now works as a prekindergarten teacher. In her spare time, she enjoys working in a number of different media.

Paul Pullara
Graphic Design
10 Walnut Street
Little Falls, NJ 07424

Paul Pullara interned at Walt Disney World Design and Development in Florida before graduating with honors from the School of Visual Arts in New York City in 1980. He has run his own graphic design studio since 1982, handling work in almost all areas: logos, corporate identity, booklets, brochures, catalogs, packaging, posters, illustration, hand lettering, and promotional and advertising design.

Randall Rayon
322 West 57th Street
New York, NY 10019

After graduating from Washington University in St. Louis in 1977 with a BFA, Randall Rayon worked exclusively for Neiman-Marcus in Dallas as a fashion illustrator. Since he moved to New York City in 1979, Randall has done illustrations for a number of department stores, including Bloomingdale's, Bonwit Teller's, and Macy's. His work has appeared in special promotional material for *Vogue* and *Elle*. While perfecting the techniques he's already using, Randall is also developing a more graphic collage style and exploring illustrative possibilities on a computer.

Mark Riedy
68 East Franklin
Dayton, OH 45459

Mark Riedy is the author and illustrator of Workbooks 5 through 8 in North Light Books' *Airbrush Techniques* series; artist Greg LaFever collaborated with Mark on several illustrations in the workbooks. Mark earned a BFA from the Columbus College of Art and Design, where he also taught after graduation. After working at a design studio and in an ad agency, he set up his own business in 1982. Winner of a number of awards, Mark's work is included in the *Society of Illustrators 23rd Annual*.

Lesley Schiff
20 East 80th Street
New York, NY 10021

A graduate of the Art Institute of Chicago in classical and modern painting, Lesley Schiff was the first to introduce high-tech technology into the art of painting through the Canon color laser machine. Lesley is both a commercial and fine artist. Her work is in the Permanent Print Collection of the Metropolitan Museum of Art in New York City and can be seen in ads for Calvin Klein, Diane Von Furstenberg, and Estée Lauder, and in the pages of *Fortune*, *Redbook*, and *Vogue*. Her work has been widely exhibited in Europe and the United States.

Carla Scornavacco
2425 North Neva
Chicago, IL 60635

A graduate of Triton College, Carla Scornavacco is a graphic designer with the Townsend Agency, Ltd., in the Chicago suburb of Rosemont, Illinois. The firm specializes in direct mail advertising and is a Fortune 500 company. Carla enjoys calligraphy and painting in her spare time.

Lenore Simon
3862 Mt. Acadia Boulevard
San Diego, CA 92111

Printmaker Lenore Simon completed her fourth Artist-in-Residency grant in 1988 and has received eight California Arts Council grants. After concentrating on intaglio printmaking for over twenty years, she began experimenting with other

printmaking techniques while working on a Technical Assistance grant several years ago. A member of Artists Equity since 1969, she has won numerous awards, and her work has been widely exhibited and collected. She teaches drawing at the University of California, San Diego, and in the San Diego public schools.

Welmoed B. Sisson
Flying Dutchman Design
17325 Germantown Road
Germantown, MD 20874

Welmoed Sisson founded Flying Dutchman Design in 1985 after an eight-year career as a graphic artist, illustrator, cartoonist, and designer. Her company now occupies its own two-story building and does work ranging from corporate stationery to full-color posters for both local and national clients.

John S. Slorp
Memphis College of Art
Overton Park
Memphis, TN 38112

John S. Slorp has been the president of the Memphis College of Art since 1982. For eighteen years before that, he was on the faculty of the Maryland Institute, College of Art, in Baltimore. He received both a BFA and an MFA from the California College of Arts and Crafts. When he's not devoting time to community service, he likes to paint and create calligraphy, lettering, and computer graphics.

Eugene M. Smith, Jr.
615 Locust Street
Mt. Vernon, NY 10552

Eugene Smith earned a BFA from the State University of New York at Purchase in 1988 and spent the summer at the Yale graphic design program in Switzerland. A freelance designer, Gene devotes part of his time to Bevington Design, Inc., in Long Island City, New York.

Chris Spollen
Moonlight Press
362 Cromwell Avenue
Staten Island, NY 10305

Chris Spollen has been a professional illustrator for the past fifteen years. His work has appeared in major publications for corporations and agencies worldwide. He is a graduate of the Parsons School of Design and a member of the Society of Illustrators.

Reed Sprunger
6517 Pawawna Drive
Fort Wayne, IN 46815

For five years after graduating from St. Francis College in Fort Wayne, Indiana, Reed Sprunger worked at several local advertising agencies. Starting in 1983, he went freelance, doing "just about anything that came along," including illustration, design, and comps. Now he does mostly illustration work as his client base gradually expands into other market areas.

John E. Thies
AT&T Bell Laboratories Art Studio
Reading, PA 19612

Although John Thies's art education was primarily in illustration and technical illustration at the Industrial Management Institute, his thirteen-year career as a senior designer for Bell Labs Graphic Art Studio has led him heavily into graphics. While designing brochures, displays, exhibits, and in-house literature, John says he "designs without 'tunnel vision' to give my clients the leading edge in graphic design and illustration."

Jack Tremblay
Jack Tremblay, Ink
P.O. Box 24
Rowley, MA 01969

A graduate of the University of Massachusetts in Amherst, Jack Tremblay runs his own studio, which specializes in pen-and-ink architectural illustrations. Jack is also a practicing registered landscape architect.

Charles E. Vadun
14814 Priscilla Street
San Diego, CA 92129

After graduating from East Michigan University, Charles Vadun spent the first fifteen years of his career in advertising agencies as a copywriter and creative director, winning over 300 awards. Making a major career change, Chuck began to freelance full-time after his cartoon work became syndicated through United Features. Currently, his clients include *Cosmopolitan*, *National Enquirer*, Private

Ledger Financial Services, the *Saturday Evening Post*, Security Pacific, US Air, and the *Wall Street Journal*.

Sharon Watts
201 Eastern Parkway
Brooklyn, NY 11238

Sharon Watts studied fashion illustration at Parsons School of Design in New York City, graduating in 1974. Since then, she has established a successful career as an illustrator with work for such magazines as *Brides*, *Family Circle*, and *New York Woman*. In addition to illustrating pattern magazines for *Vogue* and *McCall's*, Sharon's drawings appear in a weekly fashion column in the *New York Times*.

Maria Carmer Webb
P.O. Box 1761
Coos Bay, OR 97420

Maria Carmer Webb currently has three outlets for her energy: her private studio; the Black Cat Studio/Gallery, owned by her husband and fellow artist, Richard Webb; and Goodrich Marketing & Advertising, Inc., where she is the art director. She is a member of the American Institute of Graphic Arts and plans to work her way around the world before retiring to a houseboat.

Lee Woolery
2231 South Patterson
Kettering, OH 45409

A graduate of Columbus College of Art and Design, Lee Woolery is the author and illustrator of Workbooks

1 through 8 in the North Light Books' *Marker Techniques* series. After starting his design career at Hallmark in Kansas City, Lee learned most of his marker techniques at Wanamaker Advertising in Dayton, Ohio. He set up his own business as a freelance illustrator in 1984, and his representative is Scott Hull. Lee works for a number of national clients, such as Anheuser-Busch, NASA, Proctor & Gamble, and the Smithsonian Institute.

Angela Woolley
19518 Nashville Street
Northridge, CA 91326

Angela Woolley earned a BA in graphic design from California State University, Northridge, in 1987 and interned with Freed, Crown, Lee Publishing. Currently she works as a designer for a Los Angeles computer firm and does freelance photography and phototinting.

David Phillips Young
111C Windingway
Covington, KY 41011

David Phillips Young worked in a number of advertising agencies in Ohio before opening his own design studio across the border in Kentucky in 1987. Experienced in designing ads for magazines, newspapers, direct mail, radio, and television, David has won many local, state, and national awards for his work.

Index

Other Art Books from North Light

Graphics/Business of Art

Airbrush Artist's Library (6 in series) $12.95 (cloth)
Airbrush Techniques Workbooks (8 in series) $9.95 each
Airbrushing the Human Form, by Andy Charlesworth $27.95 (cloth)
The Art & Craft of Greeting Cards, by Susan Evarts $15.95 (paper)
The Artist's Friendly Legal Guide, by Conner, Karlen, Perwin, & Spatt $15.95 (paper)
Artist's Market: Where & How to Sell Your Graphic Art (Annual Directory) $18.95 (cloth)
Basic Graphic Design & Paste-Up, by Jack Warren $13.95 (paper)
Color Harmony: A Guide to Creative Color Combinations, by Hideaki Chijiiwa $15.95 (paper)
Complete Airbrush & Photoretouching Manual, by Peter Owen & John Sutcliffe $23.95 (cloth)
The Complete Guide to Greeting Card Design & Illustration, by Eva Szela $27.95 (cloth)
Creating Dynamic Roughs, by Alan Swann $27.95 (cloth)
Creative Ad Design & Illustration, by Dick Ward $32.95 (cloth)
Creative Director's Sourcebook, by Nick Souter and Stuart Neuman $89.00 (cloth)
Creative Typography, by Marion March $27.95 (cloth)
Design Rendering Techniques, by Dick Powell $29.95 (cloth)
Dynamic Airbrush, by David Miller & James Effler $29.95 (cloth)
Fashion Illustration Workbooks (4 in series) $8.95 each
Fantasy Art, by Bruce Robertson $24.95 (cloth)
Getting It Printed, by Beach, Shepro & Russon $29.50 (paper)
The Graphic Artist's Guide to Marketing & Self-Promotion, by Sally Prince Davis $15.95 (paper)
The Graphic Arts Studio Manual, by Bert Braham $22.95 (cloth)
Graphic Tools & Techniques, by Laing & Saunders-Davies $24.95 (cloth)
Graphics Handbook, by Howard Munce $14.95 (paper)
Handbook of Pricing & Ethical Guidelines, 6th edition, by The Graphic Artist's Guild $19.95 (paper)
How to Design Trademarks & Logos, by Murphy & Row $24.95 (cloth)
How to Draw & Sell Cartoons, by Ross Thomson & Bill Hewison $17.95 (cloth)
How to Draw & Sell Comic Strips, by Alan McKenzie $18.95 (cloth)
How to Draw Charts & Diagrams, by Bruce Robertson $24.95 (cloth)
How to Understand & Use Design & Layout, by Alan Swann $24.95 (cloth)
How to Understand & Use Grids, by Alan Swann $27.95 (cloth)
How to Write and Illustrate Children's Books, edited by Treld Pelkey Bicknell and Felicity Trotman, $22.50 (cloth)
Illustration & Drawing: Styles & Techniques, by Terry Presnall $22.95 (cloth)
Living by Your Brush Alone, by Edna Wagner Piersol $16.95 (paper)
Marker Rendering Techniques, by Dick Powell & Patricia Monahan $32.95 (cloth)
Marker Techniques Workbooks (8 in series) $9.95 each
The North Light Art Competition Handbook, by John M. Angelini $9.95 (paper)
North Light Dictionary of Art Terms, by Margy Lee Elspass $10.95 (paper)
Papers for Printing, by Mark Beach & Ken Russon $34.50 (paper)
Preparing Your Design for Print, by Lynn John $27.95 (cloth)
Presentation Techniques for the Graphic Artist, by Jenny Mulherin $24.95 (cloth)
Print Production Handbook, by David Bann $14.95 (cloth)
Ready to Use Layouts for Desktop Design, by Chris Prior $27.95 (cloth)
Studio Secrets for the Graphic Artist, by Jack Buchan $29.95 (cloth)
Type: Design, Color, Character & Use, by Michael Beaumont $24.95 (cloth)
Using Type Right, by Philip Brady $18.95 (paper)

Mixed Media

The Art of Scratchboard, by Cecile Curtis $21.95 (cloth)
Colored Pencil Drawing Techniques, by Iain Hutton-Jamieson $23.95 (cloth)
Complete Guide to Fashion Illustration, by Colin Barnes $32.95 (cloth)
The Figure, edited by Walt Reed $15.95 (paper)
Keys to Drawing, by Bert Dodson $21.95 (cloth)
Light: How to See It, How to Paint It, by Lucy Willis $24.95 (cloth)
Make Your Own Picture Frames, by Jenny Rodwell $12.95 (paper)
The North Light Handbook of Artist's Materials, by Ian Hebblewhite $24.95 (cloth)
The North Light Illustrated Book of Painting Techniques, by Elizabeth Tate $27.95 (cloth)
Oil Painting: A Direct Approach, by Joyce Pike $26.95 (cloth)
The Pencil, by Paul Calle $16.95 (paper)
Perspective in Art, by Michael Woods $13.95 (paper)
Perspective Without Pain Workbooks (4 in series) $9.95 each
Photographing Your Artwork, by Russell Hart $15.95 (paper)

To order directly from the publisher, include $3.00 postage and handling for one book, 50¢ for each additional book. Allow 30 days for delivery.

North Light Books
1507 Dana Avenue, Cincinnati, Ohio 45207
Credit card orders
Call TOLL-FREE
1-800-289-0963
Prices subject to change without notice.